Lighten Up!

Low-Fat Versions of More Than 100 of America's Best-Known, Best-Loved Recipes

Elaine Magee

A Fireside Book
Published by Simon & Schuster

To my toughest food critic, my husband, Dennis.
Your picky palate continues to keep me on my toes—
and I wouldn't have it any other way.

FIRESIDE
Rockefeller Center
1230 Avenue of the Americas
New York, NY 10020

FIRESIDE and colophon are registered trademarks
of Simon & Schuster Inc.

Designed by Laura Hough

Manufactured in the United States of America

1   3   5   7   9   10   8   6   4   2

Library of Congress Cataloging-in-Publication Data

Magee, Elaine.
Lighten up! : low-fat versions of more than 100 of America's best-known,
best-loved recipes / Elaine Magee.
p.   cm.
Includes index.
1. Cookery, American.   2. Low-fat diet—Recipes.   3. Brand name products
I. Title.
TX715.M2114   1997
641.5'638—dc21   97-6942
CIP

ISBN 0-684-81494-3

Acknowledgments

I would like to thank all the newspaper and magazine editors who took time out of their very busy schedules to answer my survey questions. And I would also like to thank all the food companies that were more than happy to send or fax me their most famous recipes. This book was much easier to work on because of you. Lastly, I would like to thank all the people (in my neighborhood, family, friends, and fellow Jazzercisers) who willingly tasted and commented on most of these lightened recipes. I know a recipe is a keeper when every crumb has been licked up and a handful of tasters start begging for the recipe.

Contents

Chapter 1

The Search for the Most Famous Recipes in America

Have you ever eaten Chicago-style pizza? Deep-dish pizza, with a rich crust, tons of cheese, sausage, tomatoes drenched in olive oil —and nearly 70 grams of fat per serving. I'll show you how to make it with less than half the fat—and just as delicious.

I've been lightening up high-fat recipes for a decade now, and if I've learned anything, it's that often the best low-fat recipes start with the best high-fat recipes. You do not, therefore, set out to make low-fat pizza; rather, you seek to create a low-fat version (but just as yummy) of "regular" pizza, or in this case, "famous" pizza.

The best recipe for chocolate cheesecake I know delivers about 25 grams of fat per heavenly slice. Agony with the ecstasy. But I'll give you a version that's every bit as delightful with two-thirds less fat and three-fifths the calories.

Pizza and cheesecake are just two of the more than one hundred recipes offered in this book. All of them are significantly lighter versions of famous American dishes. How did it come about? Because I'm always looking for a low-fat cooking challenge. My ears perk up every time I hear someone say, "Oooh, I just made an incredible dish. If only it weren't so high in fat." That's when my creativity flows. That's when I roll up my sleeves and attack that high-fat recipe, applying all I've learned from years fighting the fat-in-food wars.

In my *Fight Fat and Win Cookbook*, I tackled more than sixty of the most commonly made recipes in America (based on an informal national survey I conducted). I lightened up spaghetti, macaroni and cheese, tuna casserole, tacos, and pork chops, as well as chocolate chip cookies and brownies. Having reduced our national "generic" dishes, I thought it was time to lighten up the most famous recipes in America. From eighteen prominent food companies, I solicited the top "brand name" recipes, such as Fantasy Fudge, Hershey's Deep Dark Chocolate Cake, Lipton's California Dip, Chex Party Mix, Bisquick's Cheeseburger Pie, and favorite Pillsbury Bake-Off winners. To make sure I left nothing out, I also interviewed food editors from fourteen of the biggest newspapers across the country and from two major women's magazines, asking them what they thought the most famous recipes in America were.

Before I could conduct my search for the most-loved, best-known recipes in America, I had to define the recipe criteria, of which I had only one—"famous." When interviewing the food editors, I wanted to give them some additional descriptors that might trigger a recipe idea or two. So, after consulting "Webster" and his cousin "Thesaurus," this is what I came up with:

> ***Famous recipes*** are the most acclaimed and revered recipes in recent American history. They are classics or signature recipes that are so excellent that they are favorites of generation after generation. They are the recipes that people most frequently request from food companies and editors.

I tried to reach a cross section of the country with my survey in order to get a regional as well as national flavor. As you can see from the results summarized in the chart below, we have some distinctive local dishes that are nonetheless well known throughout America. You'll notice, too, that almost half of the recipes are for desserts, which says something about our national character. A few recipes were mentioned more than once, an overlap that reassured me they truly belonged. In fact, I've included more than one version of a few recipes. For that reason—and because I've added recipes of my own choice—you'll find a few recipes in the book that aren't listed in the chart.

But a survey wouldn't be complete without you. What do *you* think are the most famous recipes in America? Are there one, two, or more that we missed this go-round? Send your suggestions, and the recipes if you have them, to me c/o Fireside Books, Simon & Schuster, 1230 Avenue of the Americas, New York, NY 10020. And who knows—we might have enough famously fabulous recipes for *Lighten Up*, Volume II!

For every recipe in the book, I provide a nutritional analysis.

Food Editors

Newspapers

WHO	FAMOUS RECIPES NAMED
Judy Walker *The Arizona Republic*	Buffalo Chicken Wings Flan
Susan Puckett, Food Editor *Atlanta Constitution*	Better-Than-Sex Cake Red Velvet Cake Pound Cake

Carol Haddix, Food Editor
Chicago Tribune
	Chicago Deep-Dish Pizza
	Shimp Dijon (from Eli's Steak House
	    —unfortunately the recipe was
	    unobtainable)

Debra Byrd, Food Editor *Contra Costa Times*	Red Velvet Cake (from the Waldorf-Astoria Hotel) Paul Prudhomme's Cajun Meat Loaf
Dotty Griffith, Lifestyles Editor *Dallas Morning News*	Fettuccine Alfredo Chicken-Fried Steak with Creamy Gravy Crème Brûlée
John Kessler, Food Editor *Denver Post*	Green Chili
Britt Owen *Kansas City Kansan*	Green Rice
Barbara Taylor, Food Editor *Monterey Herald*	Pot Roast
Gerald Etter, Food Editor *Philadelphia Inquirer*	Sticky Buns Philly Cheese Steak Sandwich
Jane Lord, Food Editor *Portland Press Herald*	New England Clam Chowder
Joyce Gemperlein, Food Editor *San José Mercury*	Chicken Marbella (from *The Silver* *Palate Cookbook*)
San Francisco Chronicle	Better-Than-Sex Cake (two different versions)

Food Editors *(cont.)*

Newspapers (cont.)

WHO	FAMOUS RECIPES NAMED
Dale Curry, Food Editor *The* (New Orleans) *Times-Picayune*	Red Beans and Rice Po' Boys (hero sandwiches)
Judith Olney, Food Editor *Washington Times*	Mom Magee's Chewy Chocolate Cookies

Magazines

Good Housekeeping	Crème Brûlée Tiramisù Quiche Lorraine Philadelphia Steak Sandwich
Woman's Day	Buffalo Chicken Wings Cheesecake Baked Beans Macaroni and Cheese

Other Ideas: Famous Classic Recipes

WHO	FAMOUS RECIPES NAMED
	Focaccia Cheese Soufflé French Onion Soup Key Lime Pie Caesar Salad (from Fog City Diner in San Francisco) Eggs Benedict Mock Veal Parmigiana Belgian Waffles French Crêpes Fancy Department Store Blueberry Muffins (from *The King Arthur Flour 200th Anniversary Cookbook*) Oysters Rockefeller Award-Winning Chili

Other Ideas: Famous Classic Recipes *(cont.)*

WHO	FAMOUS RECIPES NAMED
	French Fries
	Onion Rings

Food Companies

WHO	FAMOUS RECIPES NAMED
Bacardi	Bacardi Rum Cake
Best Foods/Hellmann's (CPC International Incorporated)	Classic Creamy Potato Salad Classic Macaroni Salad Hot Artichoke Dip Spinach Dip Lemon Meringue Pie
Borden (Eagle Brand)	Magic Cookie Bars (also known as Seven-Layer Magic Cookie Bars)
Campbell's Soup Company	Green Bean Bake Simple Salisbury Steak
C&H Sugar Company	Vanilla Buttercream Frosting Crisp Cookie Cutouts Pound Cake
Crisco	Crisco Pie Crust Crisco Biscuits The Ultimate Chocolate Chip Cookie
General Mills, Incorporated	Bisquick Impossible Pie Snickerdoodles Chocolate Crinkle Cookies Lemon Squares Velvet Crumb Cake (first introduced in 1951 and still a big favorite) Lemon Chiffon Cake (this revolutionary baking discovery was introduced by Betty Crocker in 1948)
Heinz	Sweet 'n' Sour Meatballs
Hershey Foods Corporation	Deep Dark Chocolate Cake (their most-requested recipe) Hershey's Best Brownies

Other Ideas: Famous Classic Recipes *(cont.)*

WHO	FAMOUS RECIPES NAMED
Kahlúa	Kahlúa Pecan Pie Chocolate Kahlúa Cheesecake
Kellogg's	Rice Krispies Treats Oven-Fried Chicken
Kraft	Gelatin Poke Cake Cheesy Brunch Casserole Fantasy Fudge Philly 3-Step Cheesecake Velveeta Salsa Dip Cheeseburger Rice
Lipton	Lipton California Dip Onion-Roasted Potatoes Cheddar Potato Gratin
Nestlé Food Company	Libby's Famous Pumpkin Pie Libby's Pumpkin Pecan Bread Chocolate Lover's Frosting
Pillsbury Bake-Off Favorites	Orange Kiss-Me Cake (a 1950 recipe that is still popular)
Pillsbury Bake-Off Favorites *(cont.)*	Tunnel-of-Fudge Cake Cherry Winks Black-Bottom Cupcakes Peanut Blossoms
Sun Diamond Growers	Classic Oatmeal Raisin Cookies
Quaker Oats Company	Quaker Meat Loaf Choc-Oat-Chip Cookies
Ralston Purina Company	Original Chex Party Mix Muddy Buddies

I'll tell you how many calories the lightened version has, how many grams of fat per serving it contains, and the percentage of calories that comes from fat. And purely for shock value, I also include the calories, milligrams of cholesterol, and grams of fat found in a serving of the original recipe. But be assured that each recipe tastes as good as the original.

One editor I spoke with complained that "the problem with most light cookbooks is you only find a few recipe gems within each of them." This cookbook is different. Here you'll find only winners. I speak with confidence, because I tested all the recipes with as many impartial tasters as I could find. Many were tried out on the willing men and women in my Jazzercise class. Trouble was, every time I brought something in, they wanted copies of the recipe. It's a little intimidating to tell a room filled with hungry and sweaty exercisers, "Sorry, you have to wait a year for the cookbook to come out."

Well, the wait is over, and I hope you like the recipes as well as these fine (and patient) people did.

Chapter 2

The Art and Science of Cooking Light

It's easy to make food taste good when you can add lots of rich and fatty ingredients such as cream, butter, olive oil, cheese, sausage, and bacon. But how to make food taste just as good without all the fat and fatty ingredients? Ah, now there's the rub, a challenge I happen to delight in. The following pages are an attempt to encapsulate all that I've learned over the past ten years of experimenting in my kitchen trying to meet those challenges.

In order to cook tasty and tempting low-fat cuisine, you'll need to learn a few new tricks and techniques. You'll also need an array of tools (both food products and kitchen equipment) to make the task easier. First, however, you should understand the principles of lowering fat in recipes and the five functions of fat.

Making Low-Fat as Painless as Possible

I lighten up recipes operating under three general principles:

- There is an ideal level of fat that maintains a recipe's taste and textural integrity, below which the recipe will not taste the same or be as satisfying.
- There is an ideal fat replacement ingredient or combination of ingredients for every recipe that will complement the other ingredients favorably.
- The taste of any recipe is equal to the sum of its parts. In other words, start with the best-tasting, freshest individual ingredients you can find. Use fresh garlic—it tastes better than garlic powder. Use fresh herbs when you can—they have more flavor than the dried. Use the best-tasting orange juice or yogurt as fat replacements. Use the creamiest light sour cream, the sharpest reduced-fat Cheddar cheese, and so forth, and your lower-fat dish will be more likely to pass muster with the masses.

Less Means More

You are probably going to have to cook with a lot less fat than you're used to. But in this case, less is more. When you cook with *less* fat, you need to cook with *more* of other ingredients that help replace the qualities of the lost fat while adding flavors that complement the other ingredients in the original recipe. After a decade of lightening up recipes, I've come to appreciate that there truly is an art and science to cooking light.

Don't worry, I'm not going to leave you stranded in your low-fat kitchen. I've condensed all that I've learned into what I call "The Five Fs." I've also included a special section on low-fat table tips and tricks.

Let's Face It—Fat Is in Recipes for a Reason

In most cases, you can't expect to take all the fat out—remove all the fat-intensive ingredients—and still have food that looks and tastes like the original. Consider the functions of each fat-containing ingredient before you attempt to change a recipe. Only after you do that can you find your ideal lower level of fat and choose your ideal fat replacement. Fat basically has five functions.

#1   ***Fat adds flavor*** (for example, butter in a cake batter or olive oil in pesto). So add other ingredients that give a flavor boost. There are many intensely flavored foods with little or no fat. Actually, fat molecules are too big to be processed by the taste buds. But fat serves as a solvent for smells, or odorants (olfactory molecules), that *are* perceived from the back of the mouth up to the nasal receptors. We don't realize it, but smelling is an important part of tasting.

      Why do fried foods taste so good when the oil or shortening used to fry the food doesn't necessarily have a lot of flavor? There are volatiles in food released in the frying process that we find appealing, along with any browning and caramelization that take place, also adding flavor. Also, many of our favorite fats (olive oil, butter, sesame oil) have impurities in them that give them their distinctive flavors.

#2 *Fat tenderizes and moistens food* (for example, oil in muffins). In many cases (even in baking), you can replace some or all of the fat with something else that adds moisture. Ingredients such as flavored yogurts, fat-free cream cheese, light sour cream, applesauce, liqueurs, and so on all help serve this purpose in baked recipes.

You can use low-fat or fat-free marinades or salad dressings to add flavor to and tenderize lean meats. The true tenderizing agents in marinades are acid ingredients such as lemon juice, vinegar, beer, or wine. So what little oil you do add, make it a highly flavorful one—such as extra-virgin olive oil, sesame oil, or chili oil.

#3 *Fat conducts heat in sautéing and frying and lubricates cookware* (for example, sautéing peppers and onions in butter or margarine). Liquids conduct heat too. You can use low-fat liquids instead of fat or switch to cooking methods that don't involve sautéing or frying. High-quality nonstick cookware can help you cut the fat, because it doesn't require as much fat to lubricate the cookware and prevent sticking. Nonstick cooking sprays help lubricate bakeware and cookware with a minimal amount of fat by allowing you to spray tiny particles of fat onto the cooking or baking surface. I suggest using both options—that is, coating the highest-quality nonstick cookware or bakeware with nonstick cooking spray.

#4 *Fat binds, separates, and seals ingredients* (for example, egg yolks bind the fatty ingredients with the nonfatty ingredients in a cookie dough). The trick is in knowing how much fat is absolutely necessary to bind, separate, and seal ingredients. Usually you can get along just fine with less.

#5 *Fat makes food appealing because it enhances the "mouth-feel" of the food (it helps food feel good in your mouth) and the satiety (feeling of fullness and satisfaction) it produces.*

(Fat in food helps us feel fuller longer. Fat in the stomach helps delay the movement of the meal into the intestinal area.) But "mouthfeel" may not be as important to the overall enjoyment of foods as previously thought. More research needs to be done in this area.

But remember Mom Magee's Law: There are very few functions of fat that can't be performed by something else.

The Keys to Low-Fat Cooking Success

Let's summarize what we've covered so far:

- Low-fat cooking is *not* nutrition at any cost. Taste and pleasure should *not* be compromised.
- Review the functions of each fatty ingredient before you make changes. When fat serves an irreplaceable function, you'll probably need to keep *some* of it in.
- Substitute reduced-fat ingredients and products when appropriate.
- Change to a cooking method that eliminates the need for cooking fat (e.g., broiling, roasting, poaching, steaming). When it's necessary to maintain the character of the food, do use a cooking method that involves fat—just use less of it (e.g., oven frying, sautéing, pan frying, browning).

We'll expand on these points later in the chapter, but first, let's consider two simple examples of how to reduce fat but still keep the taste.

Fat Replacement Magic—Two Examples
Mascarpone Cheese

The first time I ever tried mascarpone cheese was when I read the tiramisù recipe that I chose to lighten up for this cookbook. Tiramisù was one of the dishes mentioned by a magazine food editor I interviewed for the Famous Recipes Survey, so I set out to my neighborhood supermarket to find mascarpone. When I located the said tub of mascarpone, the first thing I did was check out the nutrition information label, a little habit I've developed over the years.

I don't know if I was more surprised to read it had 13 grams of fat per ounce or more shocked to taste its mild lackluster flavor. It had the texture of semi-melted cream cheese and a taste like lightly sweetened ricotta cheese. I mean, at 13 grams of fat a pop —it had better taste like chocolate!

It didn't take much to make me decide to create my own mascarpone look- and taste-alike, which uses common ingredients that also happen to be low in fat. When you pull together light or fat-free cream cheese, low-fat ricotta, corn syrup, sugar, flour, and vanilla, and with a touch of your finger, whip them in a food processor, they transform into a low-fat "mascarpone" cheese.

Classic Piecrust

The mark of a good piecrust is how flaky it is. And what makes it flaky? Fat—to the tune of 17 grams of fat per small serving (one-twelfth of a two-crust nine-inch pie), not including the filling! So when I took on the challenge of lightening Crisco's famous piecrust recipe, I have to admit, I didn't have high hopes.

I had to cut down on the amount of shortening used, but not so much that the flakiness and piecrust texture were compromised. I settled on 5 tablespoons of shortening for 1⅓ cups flour, down from 8 tablespoons. I added 3 tablespoons of nonfat cream cheese, to be cut into the flour along with the shortening. I played around with these ingredients a few times, making everything from quiche to lemon meringue, but my crust still wasn't as flaky as the original recipe. Then it hit me. What if I added low-fat buttermilk to the flour-shortening mixture instead of water? Would the acidic buttermilk, because of its thicker texture and more complex composition, somehow keep the dough from softening and losing its flakiness? I remembered a food chemistry basic, that water plus flour equals bread, and bread is anything but flaky. So maybe if I got away from the water, I could keep my crust flaky. I tried the buttermilk, and bingo! The dough was a bit crumbly when I rolled it out, and I needed to use my hands to press the dough pieces together into a ball. But the end result was a flaky piecrust that looked and tasted just like the original—I kid you not.

Even though I was only able to cut the shortening by 3 tablespoons in a one-crust pie, it made quite a difference in calories and grams of fat per serving. I was able to cut the fat in the two-crust pie from 17.5 grams per serving to 11 grams. And the calories went from 252 to 200.

If It's All the Same to You

Ultimately, you decide how you want to cut the fat. There are many different ways to cut the fat in a recipe. For example, you can switch from regular to light mayonnaise, and if you use the same amount called for in the recipe, you will cut the fat from mayonnaise in half. Or you can use regular mayonnaise but use half as much. It's the same difference in terms of fat grams. You can make a low-fat gravy that tastes great, or you can make the same high-fat gravy you've always made but just serve less. Personally, I prefer to use the light and lower-fat products, and to create lower-fat gravies, for example, as long as they taste terrific.

Lower-Fat Cooking Methods

How you cook can be as important as what you cook. Often you can switch from a higher-fat cooking method to one of the lower-fat techniques listed below and obtain the same results with less fat. For example, instead of deep-frying, oven-fry; instead of sautéing, simmer.

BRAISING: Food is cooked over low heat in a small amount of liquid in a covered pan.

BROILING/GRILLING: This is great for higher-fat meats. Direct heat is used to cook the food, with no cooking fat required. An added benefit is that some of the fat from the meat itself can drain off during the cooking.

LIGHT BROWNING (VS. BROWNING IN A LOT OF FAT): Brush a small amount of fat in the pan or generously coat the pan with one of the nonstick cooking sprays. Cook as directed in the recipe.

OVEN-FRYING: "Frying" refers to cooking food in fat over high heat, usually in a deep-fat fryer or in a frying pan. One sure way to lose a lot of the fat is to trade in your frying pan for a cookie sheet and turn on your oven instead of your stove. Brush the food (such as egg rolls, chicken strips) lightly with oil or coat it generously with nonstick cooking spray, and bake in a moderately hot oven.

POACHING: This is great for seafood, poultry, and fruit. Poaching means cooking food in a pan of simmering liquid. It's important to cover the pan during poaching, because the steam that forms bastes the food. Poach your food in liquids that add flavor, such as broth, fruit or vegetable juice, water flavored with lemon juice or seasoned with herbs and spices, or wine (use sweet wine for fruit).

ROASTING: This cooking method doesn't need any added fat. And usually fat drains off meats during roasting. Roasting amplifies the natural flavors of foods. Often, all you add to the food being roasted is a light brushing of oil (or a combination of oil and balsamic vinegar, juice, or another liquid), or wine, or a misting with nonstick cooking spray.

SIMMERING: Instead of sautéing your food in fat, you can simmer it in a flavorful nonfat liquid, such as wine, beer, broth, or juice.

SMOKING: If you have a smoker, or if you can use your outdoor grill for smoking, you can add an incredible flavor to meats and meat dishes just by smoking them. Charcoal and wood chips are used to create smoke, which imparts a distinctive flavor to the food as it cooks. A bowl of water can be set above the charcoal to create steam, helping maintain moisture in the food being smoked.

STEAMING: This is great for vegetables. Usually, when food is being steam-cooked, it is cooked on a rack (or in a colander) in a covered pan over boiling water, which produces steam.

How Low Can You Go?

How much can you cut the fat and still maintain the taste and texture of your original recipe? Each different type of recipe definitely has an ideal fat threshold—the minimum of, for example, oil, butter, margarine, or other shortening needed to produce a recipe that still tastes like its fat-laden original.

The other day, I tried some very-low-fat desserts at a local supermarket bakery. They tasted about as good as you might imagine a brownie with only 2 grams of fat would taste. They were okay. But "okay" isn't good enough for me. My recipes need to be "great!" and "fabulous!" If it takes a couple more grams of fat for a brownie to achieve this level of taste satisfaction—then so be it. That's what you'll find in the recipes here.

I always go as far down in fat and calories as I can without compromising flavor and texture. Some of the lighter recipes for this book turned out to be especially low in fat, others had a little more. But they *all* have at least 50 percent less fat than the original recipe, and they *all* taste terrific!

During my ten years of service to the low-fat cause, I have come up with ideal fat thresholds and fat replacements for various types of recipes. They're listed in the table on pages 21–22.

Ideal Fat Thresholds and Fat Replacements for Different Types of Recipes

The ideal fat threshold is the minimum of oil, butter, margarine, shortening, or other fat-containing ingredients generally needed to produce a recipe that tastes as if it's high in fat.

Ideal fat replacements are the fat-free or lower-fat ingredients best used to replace the fat removed from a recipe.

RECIPE	FAT THRESHOLD	FAT REPLACEMENTS
Biscuits	4 tablespoons shortening for every 2 cups flour	Fat-free cream cheese, nonfat or light sour cream, or flavored low-fat yogurt
Cake Mixes	No additional fat is needed, since most mixes already contain 4 grams fat per serving; replace the oil that is to be added with one of the fat replacements listed.	Nonfat or light sour cream, applesauce, pineapple juice, or flavored yogurt, depending on the cake
Homemade Cakes and Coffee Cakes	¼ to ⅓ cup shortening or butter per cake	Liqueur for some cakes, light sour cream or low-fat vanilla yogurt for chocolate ones; fruit purees work well with carrot, apple, and spice cakes
Cheese Sauce	No butter is needed, so omit the butter if it is called for—the cheese is the vital fatty ingredient; use a sharp reduced-fat Cheddar.	Make your thickening paste by mixing the flour with a little bit of milk, then whisk in the remaining milk called for in the recipe.
Cookies	Generally you can only cut the fat by half. If the original recipe calls for 1 cup of butter, for example, try cutting it to ½ cup.	Fat-free cream cheese for rich cookies; some fruit purees may work in fruit/drop cookies

Ideal Fat Thresholds and Fat Replacements for Different Types of Recipes *(cont.)*

RECIPE	FAT THRESHOLD	FAT REPLACEMENTS
Frosting	Cut the fat by half for a buttercream frosting.	I like to use all I Can't Believe It's Not Butter Light instead of all butter.
Marinades	1 tablespoon oil per cup of marinade (or none at all)	I like to use fruit juices or beer to help balance the sharpness of the more acid ingredients in a marinade, such as vinegar or tomato juice.
Muffins and Nut Breads	2 tablespoons oil for a 12-muffin recipe	Fat-free sour cream, low-fat flavored yogurts, fruit purees
Pie and Other Pastry Crusts	3 tablespoons shortening/butter for every 1 cup flour	Use fat-free cream cheese and substitute lowfat buttermilk for the water called for.
Tomato Sauce	About 1 tablespoon olive oil for every 1½ cups sauce (very little oil is needed, since the predominant flavors come from the tomato, herbs, and spices)	None needed
Vinaigrette Dressings	1 to 2 tablespoons olive oil per ½ cup dressing	Nonalcoholic beer; wine or Champagne; fruit juice; fruit purees (raspberry or pear works well)
White Sauces and Gravies	1 teaspoon butter per serving of sauce	I just add a little more milk; I like to use whole milk for a rich white sauce because, to me, whole milk *is* cream.

Kitchen Tools—The Bare Minimum
Start with High-Quality Nonstick Pans

High-quality nonstick pans allow you to cook with little or no fat. You can even sauté food using much less fat than with ordinary pans. But some nonstick pans leave a little to be desired. Some smoke, others burn food more easily, and some nonstick coatings start peeling away within a few months of use. *Cook's Illustrated* magazine rated nonstick skillets from six leading cookware companies. They sent a set of each of the pans to six restaurant chefs and asked them all to prepare a variety of specified dishes and to incorporate the pans into the kitchen's daily food preparation for three months. The chefs considered design, construction, even heat conductivity, and performance of the nonstick surface (both release ability and durability).

Based on how the chefs evaluated the skillets, only two were recommended, the All-Clad nonstick stainless 10-inch frying pan and the Calphalon professional nonstick 10-inch omelette pan. The All-Clad pan finished slightly ahead of the Calphalon, but the Calphalon pan cost $22 less than the All-Clad pan ($58 versus $80). The four skillets that were not recommended were: Circulon 10-inch open French skillet, Scanpan 2001+ 10¼-inch frying pan/omelette pan, Le Creuset traditional frying pan, and Farberware Millennium 10½-inch sauté pan.

For Food to Be Doubly Nonstick—Use Nonstick Cooking Spray Too

Even with the best nonstick pans, it's best to use nonstick cooking sprays to keep food from sticking and to help it brown nicely. I also use nonstick cooking spray for oven frying, when I actually spray it directly on the food. I coat baking pans, casserole dishes, cookie sheets, and waffle irons with nonstick cooking spray.

I tried without success to find a spray bottle that would spray small quantities of oil on a food or pan in order to cover a large surface with a little amount of fat. The next best thing is nonstick cooking sprays. I use canola oil nonstick cooking spray when I don't want to add any particular flavor, and I use olive oil nonstick spray when the olive oil flavor would complement the flavor of the food.

Double Boiler
When you reduce or eliminate butter and egg yolks or use milk in place of cream in a custard or sauce recipe, the mixture becomes more fragile. Many times while working on recipes for this cookbook, I found I got the best results using a double boiler when thickening a mixture instead of the saucepan called for in the original recipe.

Garlic Press
Garlic is one way to add flavor to food without adding fat. And fresh is best. A garlic press makes it easy to add fresh garlic. Just peel and press!

Citrus Zester
Another way to add extra zip to a recipe is to add finely grated lemon or orange zest (the colored part of the peel). A little tool called a zester makes it really easy to do so. I chop the shavings with a knife when I'm adding the zest to batters, so I don't get a long thread of zest in one bite.

Cushionaire Cookie Sheets, Jelly-Roll Pans, and Cake Pans
When you change the fat content of a batter or dough, you also change the way heat is conducted throughout the food. I found the best results (even heat distribution and less burning) when using the Cushionaire bakeware line. I spray the pans generously with nonstick cooking sprays when appropriate.

Measuring Spoons
In low-fat cooking, fats, oils, and fat-containing ingredients are added in small but exact measurements. Use the lines on sticks of

shortening and butter wrappers when possible. But for oils and other ingredients, you'll need a set of measuring spoons.

Good Mixer

A good mixer is obviously better than a bad mixer any day of the week. But when cooking low-fat food, you will rely even more on your mixer—for example, to whip air into your batter (with less fat) and blend cookie ingredients thoroughly (with less egg yolk). Low-fat batters are usually less forgiving than high-fat ones.

Good Food Processor or Blender

I use my two food processors (I have a small food processor for small jobs) and my blender all the time. When cooking low-fat, you will want to make your own purees or similar mixtures at times, because the store-bought versions contain too much fat or don't have as much flavor as the homemade versions. You'll find this to be true, for example, with pesto and creamy salad dressings. Or for another example, you can blend a mixture of mashed potatoes and milk to replace the cream in a cream soup recipe.

Sifter

I think it's especially important in low-fat cooking to pay attention to decorating details and garnishing. If the eyes are attracted, the taste buds will be more likely to have an open mind. Frosting is eliminated in many low-fat recipes to help cut down on fat and calories. In its place, powdered sugar or cocoa or ground chocolate can be sifted onto the cake or other dessert item.

Egg Separator

It's the egg yolk that contains the fat and cholesterol, but in many recipes you can get by with only one or two yolks instead of the number called for in the original recipe. Egg whites or fat-free egg substitute replace the yolks removed from the recipe. Often I use whipped egg whites to add lightness and fluff to recipes. For all these reasons and many more, an egg separator comes in handy.

Food Tools
My Favorite Fat Replacements

The foods listed here are "must-haves" in my kitchen, because they constitute my fat replacement arsenal. These foods have one key characteristic in common—they all add flavor and moisture with little or no fat.

I believe there is an ideal fat replacment for each recipe. The foods listed here, alone or in combination, usually do the job. For example, I might use lemon yogurt as a fat replacement in corn bread or yellow cake, and maple syrup as a fat replacement when making chicken sausages. I tend to use light sour cream as a fat replacement in brownies, but I prefer to use fat-free cream cheese as a fat replacement in cookies. I might use coffee liqueur as a fat replacement in a graham cracker piecrust, but use buttermilk as a partial fat replacement in a pastry piecrust.

Buttermilk

Buttermilk makes a nice fat replacement in certain recipes because it is thick and adds a distinctive pleasantly sour flavor. I always buy the smallest container, because it tends to spoil rather quickly.

Chocolate syrup

While it may sound high in fat, chocolate syrup is virtually fat-free and contains around 40 to 50 calories per tablespoon. Use it instead of some of the oil in cakes or instead of some of the butter in brownies.

Cream cheese (fat-free)

Fat-free cream cheese makes a nice replacement for butter or shortening when the thick richness of fat is crucial, as is the case with cookies, rich cakes, frostings, piecrusts, or biscuits.

Flavored low-fat yogurt

I like to use flavored low-fat yogurt as a fat replacement for oil in quick breads and sometimes cake and coffee cakes. You can have a lot of fun with the different flavors available too—try coffee or vanilla yogurt in a chocolate cake or lemon yogurt in a spice cake.

Light or fat-free sour cream
I use light sour cream as a fat replacement for butter or shortening in cakes and brownies.

Lemon juice
I like to use lemon juice in place of most of the oil in marinades or salad dressings, because it packs a lot of flavor in a small amount.

Fruits and fruit purees, such as applesauce, and crushed fruit, such as crushed pineapple
I use crushed fruit or fruit purees when their flavors complement the other ingredients in a particular recipe—for example, crushed pineapple in place of some of the oil in a carrot cake or applesauce instead of butter or shortening in a coffee cake.

Fat-free, reduced-fat, or light mayonnaise
There are times when I use low-fat mayonnaise in place of fats or oils, particularly in cases when you need something that will coat or stick to a food (or help a crumb coating adhere, as is the case with oven-fried chicken breast), or when thickening is needed (as in a reduced-fat creamy salad dressing).

For the Caesar salad dressing in this cookbook, I needed to add something that would help carry the strong flavors in the dressing, not compete with them. So I used reduced-fat mayonnaise. When blended with the other ingredients, it produced a smooth, creamy, and emulsified mixture.

Maple syrup
I have used maple syrup instead of lard in chicken sausages and in place of oil in spice cakes and quick breads.

Molasses

Substitute molasses for some of the butter in a caramel corn recipe. It can also replace oil or butter in some meat marinades or sauces. Molasses can also be used as a replacement for some of the butter or oil in quick breads, coffee cakes, and spice cookies.

Corn syrup

You can reduce the amount of granulated sugar called for in baking recipes and then replace some of the fat with corn syrup. There's something about the construction of corn syrup that makes it hold on to its moisture in a batter longer. It actually releases its moisture slowly, over time, into the food.

My Favorite Lower-Fat Ingredients

FOR:	I LIKE TO USE:
Whipping cream, liquid	Half-and-half or whole milk, depending on the richness needed in the recipe
Whipping cream, whipped	Light Cool Whip for some recipes, but when real whipped cream is *really* necessary, I use the real thing and stretch it with whipped egg whites or get by with much less.
Half-and-half	Whole milk (To someone like me, whole milk *is* cream; I reach for whole milk when creaminess is crucial, as in Alfredo sauce, caramel sauce, creamy soups, and custards.)
Whole milk	Low-fat milk
Sour cream	Light sour cream
Cheese	Reduced-fat cheese (I love Cracker Barrel Light Sharp Cheddar)

My Favorite Lower-Fat Ingredients *(cont.)*

FOR:	I LIKE TO USE:
Eggs	Fat-free egg substitute—I use fat-free egg substitute for some or all of the eggs called for, depending on the recipe.
Mayonnaise	Light mayonnaise mixed with fat-free mayonnaise, light sour cream, or low-fat yogurt. Light mayonnaise should be used when the taste of mayonnaise is very important. In strongly flavored dishes, you can try nonfat mayonnaise. But I've found the best results blending light mayonnaise with some nonfat mayonnaise so I get a mayonnaise with less than 3 grams of fat per tablespoon but one that doesn't go all the way to zero fat— and zero taste.

Lower-Fat Cooking Tips and Tricks
The Nutritional Cost of Those "Baking Extras"

Baking purists might say, "What's a chocolate cookie without nuts?" or "What's carrot cake without coconut?" But what do these little extras *really* cost us? Just how decadent *is* the baker who decides to add some chocolate chips to his or her oatmeal cookie dough or top pumpkin pie with pecans?

It's all a matter of gastronomy philosophy, really. Some might embrace the ideology that "you're already blowing it by eating the cookie or chocolate truffle, so why not go all the way and roll it in nuts?" Others believe that every little bit counts, and any amount of calories and grams of fat you can shave off is more than welcome! I tend to subscribe to the latter view.

Many times baking recipes list one or two ingredients as "optional." I always wonder, just how optional is optional? Will the bread, cake, or cookies fall flat or taste bland without it? Can I substitute something lower in fat, such as raisins or miniature marshmallows, for high-fat ingredients, such as nuts or chocolate chips?

And then there are those "extra" ingredients. These are the items that, although required by the almighty recipe, you could probably do without—or at least replace with something lower in fat and calories. Usually both "extra" and optional ingredients are used in one of three ways: they're either on top, on the outside, or mixed into the finished batter or dough.

The popular holiday thumbprint cookie demonstrates the first two possibilities. Each cookie ball is usually rolled in chopped nuts and then the space in the center, the thumbprint, is filled with a teaspoon of jam or chocolate fudge frosting. Chocolate chips or nuts mixed into a basic oatmeal cookie dough are an example of the third.

Recipes usually call for at least half a cup of these baking extras, so in most cases that's the amount I used to compare their fat and calorie contributions in the table on pages 32 and 33.

When you study this table, it becomes quite clear that half a cup of nuts is not to be taken lightly. If you rolled your cookie balls or truffles in a quarter cup of cocoa or powdered sugar instead of half a cup of nuts, you would save more than 300 calories and over 30 grams of fat. And if you added half a cup of raisins to your coffee cake, nut bread, or oatmeal cookie dough instead of nuts, you would lower the calories by 120 and the grams of fat by more than 35.

If you love nuts and loathe raisins, you can still add nuts—just use less. To help make a little go farther, toast the nuts before adding them into the batter—it will bring out their flavor. Using a quarter cup of nuts instead of half a cup will of course cut the calories and grams of fat from that ingredient by half. And often nuts aren't *really* necessary and can be left out completely, as with zucchini bread, chocolate chip and oatmeal cookies, or muffins.

After I discovered how much dietary damage an innocent

handful of chocolate chips can do (½ cup = 430 calories and 30.5 grams of fat), it will be a while before you catch me with chocolate chips in my oatmeal cookies! If you add a cup of raisins to oatmeal cookie dough instead of chocolate chips, you lower the calories by 364 and the grams of fat by 60. And decorating cupcake tops with a cup of miniature marshmallows instead of M& M's will save approximately 640 calories and 36 grams of fat.

The Chocolate Lover's Salvation—Cocoa

If I told you that you could add the flavor of chocolate to your baking and dessert recipes without all the fat by using a new product, essentially "defatted" chocolate, now available at your supermarket, wouldn't you want to rush out and buy a great big box of this amazing stuff?

Well, guess what? Defatted chocolate isn't new at all. In fact, it's been on the market for more than a hundred and sixty years. This magical, potent powder is nothing more than your standard box of cocoa! Many health cookbooks suggest replacing each ounce of baking chocolate in recipes with three tablespoons of cocoa and one tablespoon of oil. This popular healthful cooking tip may lower saturated fat, but I'm afraid the calories and total grams of fat will be the same. Because when you do this, you are simply replacing the fat from chocolate with fat from oil.

But three tablespoons of cocoa has only 42 calories and 3 grams of fat. In comparison, an ounce of baking chocolate has 143 calories and 15 grams of fat. In a recipe that calls for four ounces of chocolate, this can make an impressive difference. You would save 404 calories and 48 grams of fat! Which would you rather put in your recipe?

There are three tricks to lowering calories, saturated fat, *and* the total amount of fat when swapping a box of cocoa for that bar of chocolate:

- In certain recipes, substituting cocoa for chocolate may not work perfectly (since cocoa does have a flourlike character

The Fat and Calorie Cost of Baking "Extras"

	CALORIES	FAT (GRAMS)	% CALORIES FROM FAT
nuts (1/2 cup)			
pecans	360	36.5	85%
walnuts, chopped	379	35	78%
almonds, slivered	398	35	74%
sunflower seeds, dry-roasted	372	32	72%
chocolate (1/2 cup)			
chocolate chips, semisweet	430	30.5	57%
chocolate chips, milk	440	27	53%
M&M's, plain (3 ounces) (1/2 cup)	420	18	39%
coconut (1/2 cup)			
flaked sweetened	175	12	59%
unsweetened	257	25	82%
dried fruit (1/2 cup)			
raisins (packed)	248	0.4	1%
dates, chopped	244	0.4	1%
apricots, chopped	154	0.1	2%

that will add to the cake's doughiness). That's why it's always best to gravitate toward recipes that already call for cocoa. You can then *reduce the fat* (shortening, butter, margarine, or oil) *in the recipe* (usually by half) with a lower-fat liquid such as evaporated skim milk, light cream cheese, light sour cream, low-fat plain yogurt, 1% milk, etc.

- In many cases you can *replace each ounce of baking chocolate called for with three tablespoons of cocoa.* But instead of adding a tablespoon of oil along with every 3 tablespoons of cocoa (the substitution suggestion on the box of cocoa), add a tablespoon of an appropriate lower-fat ingredient. Depending on the recipe, this might be strong coffee, a liqueur,

The Fat and Calorie Cost of Baking "Extras" *(cont.)*

	CALORIES	FAT (GRAMS)	% CALORIES FROM FAT
oatmeal	156	2.5	15%
marshmallows, regular or flavored miniatures (½ cup = 45 miniatures)	102	0	0

For the top of cookies

	CALORIES	FAT (GRAMS)	% CALORIES FROM FAT
Hershey's kiss (1)	26	1.5	53%
chocolate frosting (1 teaspoon)	21	1	38%
jam/preserves (1 teaspoon)	18	0	0
light jam/preserves (1 teaspoon)	7	0	0

For rolling *cookies, truffles, or cheese logs in (*instead *of nuts)*

	CALORIES	FAT (GRAMS)	% CALORIES FROM FAT
unsweetened cocoa (¼ cup)	56	4	64%
powdered sugar (¼ cup)	96	0	0%
granulated sugar (¼ cup)	192	0	0%
graham cracker crumbs (¼ cup)	128	3	22%

evaporated skim milk, light cream cheese, light sour cream, or yogurt.

• Want a tiny taste of chocolate? *Sometimes all you need is a kiss of cocoa. . . .* Just sprinkle a little cocoa into your meringue cookie batter: add a quarter cup of cocoa, for example, to the egg whites after you've beaten in the sugar. You can do the same with angel food cake batter.

What about our friends the semisweet chocolate chips? Lots of luscious chocolate recipes call for these babies instead of unsweetened chocolate baking squares. The producer adds sugar and a little more cocoa butter to make semisweet chocolate from un-

Cocoa Calculations

FOR:	USE:
1 ounce unsweetened baking chocolate	3 tablespoons cocoa + 1 tablespoon lower-fat liquid*
(143 calories, 15 grams fat)	*(42 calories, 3 grams fat)*
1²/₃ ounces semisweet chocolate	3 tablespoons cocoa + 1 tablespoon lower-fat liquid* + 4 teaspoons sugar
(240 calories, 17 grams fat)	*(106 calories, 3 grams fat)*

* These nutritional calculations use coffee as the lower-fat liquid.

sweetened chocolate. Therefore, when you substitute cocoa for semisweet chocolate, you will need to calculate some sugar into the equation (and you will need less cocoa per ounce of chocolate too).

Egg Whites—Egg Yolks' Better Half

One Halloween, my husband and I thought of a great pair of party costumes: One person could dress all in yellow, write 210 (for 210 milligrams cholesterol) on his or her chest, and be the egg yolk. The other could wear white and be the egg white. And the party introduction could go something like this: "Hi, I'm an egg yolk and this is my better half—egg white. I've got all the cholesterol and fat in the family, while my wife/husband's all muscle (protein)."

It's true, when it comes to "whipping up" low-fat recipes, the egg white is definitely the better half. Not only does each egg yolk contain about 5 grams of fat and 210 milligrams cholesterol, while the white contains mainly protein, but it's the white portion of the egg that can be whipped into a stiff foam. You might be saying, "Yes, well, what's so magical about meringue?" Granted, "whipped egg whites" may not sound sophisticated, but they sure come in handy when you want to add a little fluff and tenderness to various dishes and desserts without turning to the usual fluffers like whipped cream or soft butter or margarine, which are almost 100 percent fat!

Certainly a spoonful of whipped egg whites is not going to taste like a spoonful of whipped cream, but the difference won't be so obvious when you use it to lighten up your chocolate mousse or add boiled corn syrup and flavorings to make a frosting. The difference is even less noticeable when whipped egg whites are used to add air and tenderness to cake batters instead of creamed butter or margarine.

After you realize what you'll be saving in calories, fat, and cholesterol by fluffing your desserts with egg whites, perhaps you might be a little more tolerant of any minuscule loss in taste. Two egg whites contain a grand total of 33 calories and zero fat and cholesterol. And for your trouble, you'll be gaining 7 extra grams of protein.

When egg whites are beaten with a mixer, air bubbles are whipped in. The airy new structure that is created can then be permanently set with your basic oven. Egg whites are almost all protein, and when protein is exposed to heat, it coagulates (gelatinizes) and firms, adding structure to your baked product. Sounds simple, doesn't it? But there are some hard-and-fast rules to successful egg white whipping:

- Egg whites whip best when at room temperature
- Egg whites must be separated without a speck of yolk (eggs are easier to separate if cold; then allow the whites to come to room temperature). Whites can't form a foam with egg yolk around, because fat (something egg yolks have plenty of) prevents the whites from holding air.
- Because fat sabotages the foaming process, all beaters and bowls must also be as grease-free as possible.
- Use a glass, copper, or stainless steel bowl for whipping egg

whites. Plastic tends to hold on to grease even after thorough cleaning, and aluminum can react chemically with eggs and turn them grayish.

- Stabilizing ingredients (such as salt, lemon juice, and cream of tartar) help keep the whites smooth and aerated but will also slow the whipping process, so add them just after the eggs become frothy.
- Egg whites should be beaten until foamy and fairly stiff before adding any other ingredients.
- Don't overbeat your egg whites. Exhausted egg whites will collapse and separate.

Now for a little microbiological discussion. Although the risk of eggs being contaminated by salmonella is low, raw (and cooked) eggs should always be kept refrigerated. And it is best to cook eggs (especially the yolks) so they reach a temperature of at least 160°F. Meringues that are not baked but that are cooked by beating 239°F to 242°F hot sugar syrup into the whites in a quick, steady stream (as for a foam frosting) may not be guaranteed to be safe. However, if the whites are first warmed over hot water, bringing their temperature to about 100°F, it is more likely that they will reach the safety zone when the hot syrup is added.

Fat-Free Egg Substitutes—Egg Whites in Disguise

Egg substitutes have come a long way. Many used to be just as high in fat as regular eggs, just minus the cholesterol. Today most of the egg substitutes on the market are both cholesterol-free and fat-free. What's their secret? Well, they didn't stray far from the egg itself. Most egg substitutes are mostly egg whites. But food companies are able to do to egg whites what most of us at home can only dream about. They pasteurize them, killing any lurking microorganisms, including salmonella. They add vegetable gums for thickening and stabilizing and beta carotene for color. What you get is a product that looks more like a beaten whole egg than just an egg white.

For egg dishes such as quiches, omelets, and soufflés, I find success using half real eggs and half fat-free egg substitute. For baked items such as muffins, cakes, and cookies, I often use only egg substitute. For fancier cakes and muffins, I usually use one whole egg and then egg substitute for the rest. And I usually use all egg substitute when making cookies, since my kids like to test the raw dough, and there is no threat from salmonella with pasteurized egg substitutes.

Filo . . . Nothing More Than . . . Filo

The fattiest part of a peach pie, pot pie, or quiche isn't what goes in the middle, but what's on the top and bottom—crispy crust! That decorative pastry shell is going to cost you dearly.

Many of these dishes are favorites of mine, and so I've made it my mission, over the past year, to lower the fat and calories they contain. I quickly discovered it's almost impossible to do so without losing the piecrust. So for those who think crustless quiche is like bread without butter or cold cereal without milk, have I got a crust for you! Filo. Nothing more than filo (and a little butter).

For many of us, our first introduction to filo was that sinfully sweet and buttery Greek treat called baklava. With my first taste, I mistook filo for a high-fat pastry crust. But actually there's nothing fatty about filo—at least not before it meets up with a pastry brush dripping with butter.

You see, lucky for us, the sheets of filo that you buy don't contain any butter. But most filo recipes instruct you to brush each layer of paper-thin dough with *lots* of butter. Well, guess what— you don't have to brush every sheet. You can brush every two or three sheets. And you don't have to use *lots* of butter to make a flaky, flavorful filo crust. You only need about a tablespoon of butter, margarine, or diet spread to coat a pie pan's worth of filo. A low-fat crust is only a brush away!

The filo dough that you are most likely to find in the frozen food section of your supermarket—(Athens Foods Filo Dough Leaves)—is made from flour, water, cornstarch, salt, vegetable oil, and preservatives, in that order. When there's more salt than there is oil, you know it's either very, very salty or very, very low in fat. In this case, it's the latter (each sheet of filo contains only 75 milligrams of sodium). Each sheet is virtually fat-free (0 grams of fat per ounce) and cholesterol-free, and contains about 60 calories.

Anyone who has worked with filo knows that there are a few tricks to using these thin, quick-drying sheets of pastry. The first rule is to work fast, the second is to work fast, and the third is to work fast. While you are working with a sheet or two at a time, keep a slightly damp, warm towel over the remaining sheets of filo to prevent them from drying out and cracking (making your job as pastry chef very frustrating) before they are used.

Now for the next filo challenge. Your pie pan is round and the sheets of filo are rectangular. You can either use a round platter (about 12 inches in diameter) as a guide and cut the sheets of filo into circles the right size for your standard 9-inch pie pan, or you can let part of each layer hang over the edge of the pan, alternating around the pan as you layer the dough. Once the crust is filled, this overhang can be folded over to help cover the filling. Brush with a little more butter, margarine, or diet spread to help coat and seal the top layers.

Making a Filo Crust

Defrost the filo according to the package directions. Remember, once you unwrap the filo, it's important to keep a warm, slightly damp cloth over the unused sheets.

Melt a tablespoon of butter, margarine, or diet spread. Lay two sheets of filo in a pie pan that has been generously coated with nonstick cooking spray. Lightly brush some of the melted butter over the filo, starting with the edges; then brush the sides, and finally the bottom. Lay two more sheets of filo on top and brush with about a teaspoon more butter. Finish by laying two more sheets of filo in the pie pan and brushing with the remaining butter.

Herbs and Spice and Everything Nice

Herbs and spices are even more important than usual when cooking low-fat because they are a great way to add flavor without adding fat.

When it comes to herbs and most spices, fresh is usually best. But commercially dried herbs and preground spices can certainly do the trick too. If you can get fresh herbs, keep them in the vegetable crisper and use them as soon as possible. If you know you won't need all of any herb within a few days, you can freeze some of that herb. Simply remove the leaves from the stems, spread the leaves in a single layer on a baking sheet, and set in the freezer. Once herbs are completely frozen, put them in small freezer bags. There is no need to defrost them before adding them to soups, stews, or other hot dishes.

I've gotten in the habit of using whole nutmeg, which keeps for months in the spice cabinet. Use the grater with the smallest holes you have, or a special nutmeg grater, to grate it when needed.

As for storing store-bought dried herbs and spices, here are two terrific tips:

- Purchase the herbs and spices you don't use often in small containers. For the best flavor, it's best to use ground spices within a year; herbs tend to lose their flavor even faster than spices.
- Keep herb and spice containers tightly closed and in a cool, dark, dry place. Sunlight, heat, and exposure to the air promote the evaporation of oils and flavor from the herbs and spices. A place in one of your kitchen cabinets that is away from the oven or stove will do perfectly.

You can use fresh or dried herbs interchangeably in most recipes, as long as you adjust the amount accordingly. Because dried herbs are more concentrated, you use less of the dried herb than of the fresh. In general, a half teaspoon or slightly less of the dried is equal to one tablespoon of the fresh.

I always have a jar of Italian herb seasoning blend on hand, and I like to have jars of pumpkin pie spice and lemon pepper, and perhaps a Cajun spice blend. But with a plethora of herbs and spices at your disposal, there are lots of interesting blends you can make yourself to help boost the flavor of many a low-fat dish.

Here are some of the more common herb and spice blends. You can buy some of these blends in your supermarket, but you can make any of them yourself with a blender (or mini-processor or spice/coffee grinder; just combine all the ingredients and finely grind):

BEEF BLEND: 2 tablespoons rosemary, 2 tablespoons savory, 1 tablespoon thyme, 1 tablespoon marjoram

CAJUN BLEND: 1 tablespoon chili powder, 1 tablespoon paprika, 1 tablespoon onion flakes, 1 tablespoon garlic powder, 1 tablespoon allspice, 1 tablespoon cayenne pepper, 1 tablespoon thyme

CURRY BLEND: 1 tablespoon mustard powder, 1 tablespoon ground ginger, 1 tablespoon turmeric, 1 tablespoon cumin, 1 tablespoon allspice, 1 tablespoon cayenne pepper, 1 1/2 teaspoons fennel seeds

FRENCH BLEND: 3 tablespoons dried chives, 2 tablespoons tarragon, 1 tablespoon chervil, 1 tablespoon parsley flakes

ITALIAN HERB BLEND: 1 1/2 tablespoons basil, 1 tablespoon thyme, 1 tablespoon oregano, 1 tablespoon rosemary, 1 tablespoon garlic powder, 1 1/2 teaspoons marjoram, 1 1/2 teaspoons sage, 1/2 teaspoon cayenne pepper

JAPANESE BLEND: 3 tablespoons ginger, $1\frac{1}{2}$ tablespoons garlic powder, 1 tablespoon dried lemon peel, 1 tablespoon mustard powder

MILD MEXICAN BLEND: 2 tablespoons chili powder, 1 tablespoon ground cumin, 1 tablespoon oregano, 1 tablespoon garlic powder

POULTRY BLEND: $2\frac{1}{2}$ tablespoons sage, $2\frac{1}{2}$ tablespoons thyme, 2 tablespoons marjoram

PUMPKIN PIE BLEND: $\frac{1}{4}$ cup ground cinnamon, 2 tablespoons ground or grated nutmeg, 1 tablespoon ground cloves

Other Flavoring Agents
Onion
Peppers (from bell peppers to jalapeños)
Garlic
Lemon, lime, or orange zest or peel and juice

Table Tips and Tricks

Cooking these low-fat masterpieces is only the beginning. Once they hit the table, many popular condiments and spreads can commit nutritional sabotage within a matter of seconds.

What types of fat do people add at the table? **Butter** and **margarine** top the list. Let your sticks or tubs of butter or margarine remain a permanent fixture in your refrigerator, *not* your dining room. Out of sight, out of mind: if it's there, people are more likely to use it.

When you want a low-fat spread for toast or waffles, try the better-tasting diet margarines. They're easier to spread thin, and there are a couple of good ones that have only half the fat of stick butter or margarine. I think the best-tasting two are I Can't Believe It's Not Butter light and Dairy Maid light spread (from the makers of Challenge butter).

One of my tricks for discouraging the use of butter as a spread on toast, muffins, biscuits, English muffins, or bagels is to offer homemade (reduced-sugar) jams. I've found that no one can resist homemade preserves.

Other table fats to be leery of are **mayonnaise** and **sour cream**. At 10 grams of fat per measly tablespoon, mayonnaise isn't as harmless as it looks. Switch to light or low-fat mayonnaise, whichever your family prefers. And if you like to have the mayonnaise at the table, serve it in a small bowl with the smallest serving spoon you can find. You and your family will be more likely to spread it lightly. The same goes for **tartar sauce,** which is basically dressed-up mayonnaise. There is fat-free tartar sauce available in most supermarkets, but chances are pretty good that you won't like the way it tastes. I recommend making your own, using light or low-fat mayonnaise and your favorite pickle relish, along with chopped green olives, French mustard, minced shallots, and chopped parsley.

The light sour creams on the market taste pretty good. Try serving appropriate dishes with a dollop (about two tablespoons) as garnish. I'll bet you dollars to doughnuts most people will make do with the dollop and won't go looking for more.

As I'm sure you've already discovered, there are scores of low-fat and nonfat **salad dressings** vying for your attention on the supermarket shelf. But how many taste great? The choices dwindle to a handful or less. And most of these are Italian vinaigrette-style dressings. A low-fat creamy dressing that doesn't taste like plastic is hard to come by. I prefer to make my own creamy dressing using low-fat or light mayonnaise, light sour cream, and low-fat milk. If that sounds too intimidating, then try buying the dressing mix packets for ranch dressing and other creamy dressings and adding your choice of reduced-fat mayonnaise and milk.

Putting It into Practice—Challenging Makeovers

Makeover #1 *Cut Everywhere You Can, and It Will Add Up*
                —Chicago-Style Pizza

When I think of Chicago-style pizza, I immediately think back to my days at graduate school and a certain pizza restaurant in town that served a wonderful deep-dish pizza with stewed tomatoes on top. I have fond memories not only of frequenting this restaurant with friends to celebrate everything from Friday to the end of finals, but also of the pizza itself. In fact, just the mere mention of it starts me salivating like one of Pavlov's dogs.

So imagine my horror when I analyzed a recipe of Chicago-style pizza and discovered that one serving contained 68 grams of fat! But once I looked at the original recipe again, I immediately found multiple ways to reduce the fat. You could lower the oil in the crust. You could switch to reduced-fat cheese. You could use a lower-fat sausage on top, use less of it, or use none at all and instead top the pizza with assorted vegetables. And you could brush the top of the crust with very little olive oil or simply spray it with olive oil nonstick cooking spray. And you could definitely do without the half a cup of olive oil drizzled over the top of the stewed tomatoes.

So cut wherever you can, and it will add up. My lower-fat but still delicious version contains 15.5 grams of fat and 700 calories per serving, a saving of 40 grams of fat and 375 calories per serving.

Makeover #2 *The Ultimate Cheesecake*

Just relax, close your eyes, and let your taste buds, inspired by past culinary exploits, envision the delightfully decadent dessert of your dreams. Something so rich and creamy it's sure to satisfy every chocoholic and every dessert traditionalist.

It never fails. Whenever I try this mental food fantasy, I can't seem to shake the image of a big fat slice of double-rich, double-delicious cheesecake! Not just any cheesecake—chocolate cheesecake. You might think the only place health-conscious eaters could consume an entire slice of chocolate cheesecake is fantasyland, where fat and calories evaporate into thin air. But read on.

My favorite chocolate cheesecake recipe calls for 24 ounces of cream cheese, which by itself contributes 148 calories, 47 milligrams of cholesterol, and 15 grams of fat per serving (with 16 servings per recipe). Four eggs and up to 8 tablespoons of butter are also on the standard list of ingredients. The butter adds 51 calories and 6 grams of fat per serving, and the eggs add 53 milligrams of cholesterol and a gram of fat per serving.

Are you already counting up the grams? Wait—I'm not finished. Some cheesecake recipes also call for 8 ounces of sour cream (at a cost of 30 calories and 3 grams of fat per serving). And with chocolate cheesecake, there is, of course, the nutritional cost of the chocolate to consider (4 ounces of semisweet chips will add 36 calories and 2.5 grams fat per serving).

Add all this up per slice and suddenly we're talking about a food fantasy with 20 to 26 grams of fat per serving. But with a wave of my nutritional wand, I can transform this rich dessert into one with 67 percent less fat and 40 percent fewer calories, without sacrificing that characteristically creamy texture or rich chocolate taste. We're not talking tofu here either.

#1 It's up to you, but I prefer to use half fat-free cream cheese and half Philadelphia light cream cheese (in the tub) to make my cheesecake. You can use a mixture of low-fat ricotta cheese and light sour cream instead of the fat-free cream cheese if you like.

#2 All those tablespoons of butter called for to make the crumb crust are best left in the refrigerator. Instead, generously spray the springform pan with nonstick cooking spray, then coat the pan with cookie crumbs.

#3 Of the four eggs normally called for, I use just one, because one yolk is usually enough to bind the fatty and nonfatty ingredients into a smooth batter. The rest of the yolks can be replaced by egg substitute or egg whites.

Sound too good to be true? Since seeing (and tasting) is believing, I'll share my made-over Chocolate Grand Marnier Cheesecake with you. The original recipe contained 270 calories per slice, with 63 percent calories from fat (19 grams of fat), and 101 milligrams of cholesterol. Compare that with the made-over version, still delicious, with 160 calories per serving, 39 percent calories from fat (7 grams of fat), and 22 milligrams of cholesterol.

Chocolate Grand Marnier Cheesecake

⅔ cup (4 ounces) semisweet chocolate chips
1 tablespoon 1% milk
¼ cup (about 1 ounce) crushed Nabisco chocolate Teddy
grahams (or use reduced-fat Oreos or SnackWell's
chocolate crème cookies)
Vegetable oil nonstick cooking spray
12 ounces Philadelphia light cream cheese (in the tub),
softened
12 ounces Philadelphia fat-free cream cheese (or ¾ cup
low-fat ricotta cheese blended with ¾ cup light sour
cream), softened
⅔ cup sugar
¼ cup all-purpose flour
⅛ teaspoon salt
1 large egg
½ cup fat-free egg substitute
2 tablespoons Grand Marnier (another liqueur may be
substituted)
1 teaspoon vanilla extract
Thin orange slices (optional)

Preheat oven to 325 degrees. In a small nonstick saucepan, combine the chocolate chips and milk and heat over low heat, stirring frequently, until the chocolate is fully melted and the mixture is smooth. Let cool.

In a food processor, process enough Teddy grahams to make ¼ cup crumbs. Generously coat the bottom and about 1 inch up the side of a 9-inch springform pan with nonstick cooking spray. Add the crushed crumbs to the pan and tilt to coat the bottom and 1 inch of the side.

In a large bowl, beat the cream cheeses, sugar, chocolate mixture, flour, and salt with an electric mixer on medium speed until combined. Add the egg and egg substitute and beat on low speed *just until combined.* Stir in the liqueur and vanilla. Pour the filling into the prepared springform pan.

Bake in the center of the oven for 50 to 55 minutes, or until lightly browned. Let cool on a wire rack for 20 minutes, then loosen the crust from the side of the pan with a knife if necessary.

Let cool for 30 minutes longer, then remove the side of the springform pan. Let the cake cook completely, then chill in the refrigerator for at least 2 hours. Garnish with thin orange slices if desired.

MAKES 16 SERVINGS

Nutritional Analysis per Serving:
Calories, 160; Cholesterol, 22 mg; Sodium, 176 mg
% Calories from: Protein, 14%; Carbohydrate, 47%; Fat, 39% (7 gm)

CHOCOLATE GRAND MARNIER CHEESECAKE WITH CHOCOLATE TRUFFLE TOPPING: Spread Two-Minute Chocolate Truffle Topping (recipe follows), made with Grand Marnier, evenly over the top of the cheesecake, starting in the center and ending about 1 inch from the edge. Sprinkle 2 tablespoons Chocolate Teddy Graham crumbs evenly over the chocolate topping. (This topping will add about 22 calories per serving.)

Two-Minute Chocolate Truffle Topping
¼ cup (1½ ounces) semisweet chocolate chips
3 tablespoons 1% milk (or similar)
1 tablespoon liqueur of choice (see Note)

In a small saucepan, preferably nonstick, melt the chocolate with the milk and liqueur over medium-low heat, stirring constantly, until smooth—the chocolate should be melted and the ingredients well blended. Serve warm or let cool. Pour over angel food cake, fresh fruit, or fat-free pound cake, or use as a dip for fruit.

MAKES 8 SERVINGS DESSERT TOPPING

NOTE: Think of your favorite truffle flavor. If you like Irish Crème truffles, add Bailey's or a similar liqueur. If you like Grand Marnier truffles, add Grand Marnier or another orange liqueur. And so forth.

Nutritional Analysis per Serving:
Calories, 36; Cholesterol, 25 mg; Sodium, 4 mg
% Calories from: Protein, 5%; Carbohydrate, 47%; Fat, 48% (2 gm)

Makeover #3   *Chocolate Mocha Mousse*
What's rich and French and chocolate all over? Chocolate mousse! This is no pudding either, folks. This is pure, unadulterated heaven. But this slice of heaven has its price. With an ingredients list that includes heavy cream, chocolate, and egg yolks, you can see the handwriting on the nutritional wall.

Along with a few bites of creamy, intensely rich chocolate comes a cold, cruel caloric reality. And for many of us, classic chocolate mousse can only be an occasional indulgence. Each serving of traditional chocolate mousse has about 240 to 300 calories, 16 to 22 grams of fat (about 64% calories from fat), and 150 to 200 milligrams of cholesterol. *But,* with a few carefully calculated ingredients adjustments, chocolate mousse can become a weekly treat.

#1   Instead of chocolate, use cocoa (defatted chocolate).

#2   Cut the number of yolks by half and replace the lost yolks with fat-free egg substitute.

#3   And, for my final magic trick, replace *all* of the fluff from the whipped heavy cream with whipped egg whites. You heard right, egg whites. Add a bit of strong coffee or liqueur (Bailey's Irish cream works well) for extra flavor, and you have a dessert that looks and tastes like chocolate mousse but is much, much lighter.

With these changes, you can enjoy a dessert that has only 100 calories, 2 grams of fat (13% calories from fat), and 53 milligrams cholesterol per serving.

Original Recipe Ingredients List:

2 cups milk
¼ cup sugar
3 ounces semisweet or sweet chocolate
4 egg yolks, beaten
¾ cup heavy cream
1 teaspoon vanilla

CHOCOLATE MOCHA MOUSSE (NEW AND IMPROVED VERSION)
1 envelope unflavored gelatin (scant 1 tablespoon)
*¼ cup cold strong coffee, or 3 tablespoons liqueur of your
    choice mixed with 1 tablespoon water*
6 tablespoons unsweetened cocoa
½ cup boiling-hot strong coffee
2 large egg yolks
¼ cup fat-free egg substitute
½ cup plus 2 to 4 tablespoons sugar
1 teaspoon vanilla extract
4 egg whites
*Fresh berries, light Cool Whip, or whipped cream for garnish
    (optional)*

Soak gelatin in the cold coffee until softened, about 5 minutes.
    In a large bowl, combine the cocoa with the boiling-hot coffee

and stir until smooth. Add the gelatin mixture and stir until gelatin dissolves. In a small bowl, beat together the egg yolks, egg substitute, and ½ cup sugar. Add the egg yolk mixture to the cocoa mixture and chill in refrigerator until it's about to set (pudding consistency), about 45 minutes.

Add the vanilla to the mousse mixture and whisk until light and smooth, about 1 minute.

In a large bowl, whip the egg whites until stiff but not dry. Gently fold them into the chocolate mixture along with the remaining 2 to 4 tablespoons sugar. Spoon into 6 to 8 serving cups or glasses. Chill until set, at least 1 hour.

Garnish each serving with fresh berries or a small dollop of light Cool Whip or whipped cream if desired.

MAKES 8 SERVINGS

Nutritional Analysis per Serving:
Calories, 101; Fiber, 1.5 gm; Cholesterol, 53 mg; Sodium, 73 mg
% Calories from: Protein, 13%; Carbohydrate, 74%; Fat, 13% (2 gm)

NOTE: Because of the rare possibility of salmonella contamination, raw eggs should not be consumed by young children, the elderly, or adults with an illness or suppressed immune functions.

Chapter 3

Appetizers, Dips, and Side Dishes

Extra-Creamy Coleslaw

My father loves the Kentucky Fried Chicken colesaw and in fact has ordered coleslaw in nice restaurants around the world—but none has compared, in his opinion, to KFC's version. I found a clone recipe for KFC coleslaw in the book *Top Secret Recipes* and lightened it up for him. Here it is.

> ⅓ cup sugar
> ½ teaspoon salt
> ⅛ teaspoon freshly ground pepper
> ¼ cup 1% milk
> ½ cup Best Foods Hellmann's low-fat mayonnaise
> ¼ cup low-fat buttermilk
> 1½ tablespoons white vinegar
> 2½ tablespoons lemon juice
> 8 cups very finely chopped cabbage (about 1 medium head)
> 1 cup grated carrots

In a large bowl, combine the sugar, salt, pepper, milk, mayonnaise, buttermilk, vinegar, and lemon juice and beat with an electric mixer until smooth. (Or combine in a food processor and process until smooth, then transfer to a large bowl.) Add the cabbage and carrots and toss to blend with dressing. Cover and refrigerate for at least 3 hours before serving.
MAKES 8 SERVINGS

Nutritional Analysis per Serving:
Calories, 88; Fiber, 2 gm; Cholesterol, 1 mg; Sodium, 303 mg
% Calories from: Protein, 7%; Carbohydrate, 85%; Fat, 14% (1.4 gm)

NOTE: The original clone recipe contains 163 calories, 9.5 milligrams cholesterol, and 11.5 grams of fat per serving.

Buffalo Chicken Wings

2 teaspoons Lawry's seasoned salt (or similar)
2 teaspoons chili powder
2 teaspoons garlic powder
1 teaspoon freshly ground pepper
4 teaspoons flour
2¹/₂ pounds (about 28) wing drumettes
3 tablespoons beer
1 recipe light Roquefort dressing or light Hidden Valley
*   Ranch dressing (optional)*

Blend the seasoned salt, chili powder, garlic powder, pepper, and flour on a plate. Pull off any skin from the drumettes. Add the chicken to the seasoning mixture and turn to coat well, pressing the mixture onto the chicken.

Heat a large nonstick skillet over medium-high heat. Coat generously with nonstick cooking spray. Add the chicken wings (cooking in batches if necessary) and cook for about 4 minutes, or until browned. Turn the wings over and cook for 4 minutes more. Lower the heat to medium-low and add the beer. Cover the pan and cook for about 5 minutes. Turn the wings over again and cook for 5 more minutes, or until cooked through. Serve with light Roquefort or ranch dressing if desired.

MAKES 7 SERVINGS

Nutritional Analysis per Serving (not including dressing):
Calories, 212; Fiber, 0.1 gm; Cholesterol, 92 mg; Sodium, 566 mg
% Calories from: Protein, 71%; Carbohydrate, 3%; Fat, 26% (5.8 gm)

NOTE: KFC Hot Wings contain 314 calories and 22 grams of fat per serving of 4 wings.

Creamy Green Bean Bake with Oven-Fried Onion Rings

Rich and creamy green bean casseroles appear on tables across the country at Thanksgiving. This lighter version means you can enjoy it without guilt.

2 10-ounce boxes French-style frozen green beans
1 10¾-ounce can Healthy Request condensed cream of
*   mushroom soup*
¼ cup light or nonfat sour cream
¼ cup 1% milk
1 teaspoon low-sodium soy sauce
Dash of freshly ground pepper
1 tablespoon diced pimiento (optional)
Crispy Oven-Fried Onion Rings (recipe follows)

Preheat the oven to 350 degrees. Cook the frozen beans according to the package instructions; drain well.

In a 1-quart casserole dish or a 9-inch square baking dish, combine the soup, sour cream, milk, soy sauce, and pepper, and the pimiento if using. Add the green beans and stir well.

Bake for 20 minutes, or until bubbly. Sprinkle the crispy onions over the top and bake for 5 minutes more.

MAKES 6 SERVINGS

Crispy Oven-Fried Onion Rings

1½ teaspoons oil
1 medium onion
¼ cup fat-free egg substitute
¼ cup Italian-style seasoned bread crumbs
Nonstick canola cooking spray

Preheat the oven to 350 degrees. Spread the 1½ teaspoons oil over the bottom of a 9-inch pie plate. Slice the onion and separate it into rings. Put the fat-free egg substitute in a shallow medium bowl and the bread crumbs in another shallow medium bowl. Dip the onion rings in the egg mixture, remove with a slotted spoon or your fingers, and place in the bread crumbs, turning to coat well. Place the onion rings in the prepared pan and coat the tops generously with nonstick canola cooking spray. Bake for 15 minutes. Flip the rings over and bake for 10 minutes more, or until lightly browned and crisp.

Nutritional Analysis per Serving:
Calories, 102; Fiber, 3 gm; Cholesterol, 2 mg; Sodium, 337 mg
% Calories from: Protein, 17%; Carbohydrate, 63%; Fat, 20% (2 gm)

NOTE: Original recipe contains approximately 178 calories, 3.5 milligrams cholesterol, and 12 grams of fat per serving.

Cheddar Potato Gratin

Rich Cheddar taste, stick-to-your-ribs flavor, and half the fat.

1 envelope Lipton Recipe Secrets onion soup mix
1 cup nonalcoholic beer, regular beer, or water
2 pounds all-purpose potatoes (about 3 large), thinly sliced
1½ cups (about 6 ounces) shredded reduced-fat sharp
    Cheddar cheese
3 tablespoons grated Parmesan cheese

Preheat the oven to 375 degrees. Blend the onion soup mix and beer; set aside. In a 2-quart rectangular baking dish sprayed with nonstick cooking spray, layer half of the potatoes. Pour half of the soup mixture over the potatoes and top with half of the cheese. Repeat the layering and sprinkle the Parmesan over the top.

Cover with aluminum foil and bake for 1 hour. Remove the foil and continue baking for 5 more minutes, or until the top browns slightly.

MAKES 8 SERVINGS

Nutritional Analysis per Serving:
Calories, 222; Fiber, 3 gm; Cholesterol, 13 mg; Sodium, 775 mg
% Calories from: Protein, 21%; Carbohydrate, 61%; Fat, 18%
(4.5 gm)

NOTE: Original recipe contains 266 calories, 30 milligrams cholesterol, and 9.5 grams of fat per serving.

French Onion Soup

This light version of the classic French bistro dish has less than a third of the fat and calories of the original, but it tastes so good, you'll never know what you're missing.

> 4 ounces (1 cup grated) reduced-fat Jarlsberg (or Swiss)
>   cheese
> 6 tablespoons shredded Parmesan cheese
> 1 tablespoon olive oil
> 4 large yellow onions, thinly sliced lengthwise
> 1 tablespoon minced garlic
> 1 bay leaf
> 1 12-ounce bottle nonalcoholic or light beer
> 1/2 teaspoon salt
> 1/2 teaspoon freshly ground pepper
> 1/4 cup Madeira wine
> 2 cups low-sodium chicken broth
> 1 10 1/2-ounce can condensed beef consommé
> Soup Croutons (recipe follows)

Combine the Jarlsberg and Parmesan cheeses; set aside. Heat the oil in a large nonstick soup pot or saucepan over medium-low heat. Add the onions, garlic, and bay leaf and coook until the onions begin to brown. Add 1/2 cup of the beer and cook until the onions begin to caramelize. Add the salt and pepper and continue stirring another minute. Add the wine and cook until most of it has evaporated. Add the remaining 1 cup beer and cook until the liquid is reduced by half. Add the chicken broth and beef consommé, cover, and simmer for 30 minutes. Adjust the seasoning if necessary and remove the bay leaf.

Preheat the broiler. Ladle the soup into ovenproof bowls, float 1 crouton on top of each, and sprinkle with cheese mixture. Set the bowls on a baking sheet and place under the broiler until the cheese is lightly browned and bubbling. (The cheese can also be melted in a microwave.)

MAKES 6 SERVINGS

Nutritional Analysis per Serving (including croutons):
Calories, 276; Fiber, 2.5 gm; Cholesterol, 16 mg; Sodium, 945 mg % Calories from: Protein, 22%; Carbohydrate, 50%; Fat, 28% (8.5 gm)

NOTE: Original recipe contains 800 calories, 70 milligrams cholesterol, and 30 grams of fat per serving.

Soup Croutons

6 slices sourdough or French bread (sliced on the diagonal)
Olive oil nonstick cooking spray
2 tablespoons shredded or grated Parmesan cheese

Preheat the oven to 325 degrees. Coat both sides of the bread with nonstick cooking spray. Place on a cookie sheet and sprinkle the tops with the Parmesan cheese. Bake until crisp and golden brown, about 15 minutes (check often, so the croutons don't burn).

Deluxe Baked Beans

When I started collecting people's favorite baked bean recipes, I quickly realized most are really ways to doll up canned baked beans. I was hard-pressed to find a "scratch" baked bean recipe. Well, of all the ones I collected, I liked this one the best. It's from Lottie O'Leary of Concord, California. Enjoy!

1 large yellow onion, chopped
5 strips Louis Rich less-fat turkey bacon, diced
2 16-ounce cans (or 1 32-ounce can) vegetarian baked
    beans (I prefer Bush's Best vegetarian baked beans
    with no fat)
2 to 4 tablespoons packed brown sugar (depending on your
    sweet tooth)
1 tablespoon prepared mustard
½ cup chili sauce (such as Heinz)

Preheat the oven to 350 degrees. Coat a large nonstick frying pan with nonstick cooking spray. Add the onion and bacon and cook over medium-low heat until the onion is tender and the bacon is crisp. Remove from the heat and stir in the beans, brown sugar, mustard, and chili sauce.

Spoon into a 2-quart casserole dish that has been coated with nonstick cooking spray. Bake for 35 to 45 minutes, until bubbling.
Makes 7 servings

Nutritional Analysis per Serving:
Calories, 211; Fiber, 6.6 gm; Cholesterol, 7 mg; Sodium, 975 mg
% Calories from: Protein, 18%; Carbohydrate, 74%; Fat, 8%
(1.8 gm)

NOTE: Original recipe contains 220 calories, 14 milligrams cholesterol, and 4 grams of fat per serving.

Salsa-Cheese Dip

An easy, cheesy snack with half the fat of the original recipe.

1 pound Velveeta light pasteurized process cheese product, cubed
1½ cups Pace picante sauce or salsa (or similar)
2 cloves garlic, minced or pressed
2 tablespoons chopped fresh cilantro

Combine the Velveeta and salsa in a saucepan and stir over low heat until the cheese is melted. (Or microwave the cheese and salsa in a 2-quart microwave-safe bowl on High for 5 minutes, or until the cheese is melted, stirring once after 3 minutes.) Stir in the garlic and cilantro. Serve hot, with low-fat tortilla chips or vegetable dippers.
MAKES 3½ CUPS

Nutritional Analysis per ¼-Cup Serving (not including chips or vegetable dippers):
Calories, 78.5; Fiber, 0.5 gm; Cholesterol, 11 mg; Sodium, 504 mg
% Calories from: Protein, 30%; Carbohydrate, 24%; Fat, 46% (4 gm)

NOTE: Original recipe contains 118 calories, 21 milligrams cholesterol, and 8.5 grams of fat per ¼-cup serving.

Steak Fries

Once you've tried these, you won't go back to deep-fried again.

4 medium to large russet (baking) potatoes
1 tablespoon canola oil
Canola oil nonstick cooking spray
Salt or seasoning salt (optional)

Scrub the potatoes and cut them crosswise in half. Place cut side down on a cutting board and use an apple cutter/corer to cut into wedges. Or use a sharp knife to cut into steak fries. If time permits, soak the potatoes in cold water for up to 1 hour to remove excess starch; drain and dry well.

Preheat the oven to 425 degrees. Coat the bottom of a 9 by 13-inch baking pan or a small cookie sheet with the canola oil. Place the potato wedges in the pan. Spray the tops of the fries generously with nonstick cooking spray. Bake for about 20 minutes. Flip the fries over, sprinkle with salt if desired, and bake for 10 minutes more, until lightly browned.

MAKES 4 TO 6 SERVINGS

Nutritional Analysis per Serving (6 servings per recipe, using medium potatoes):
Calories, 203; Fiber 4 gm; Cholesterol, 0 mg; Sodium, 14 mg (not including optional salt)
% Calories from: Protein, 7%; Carbohydrate, 82%; Fat, 11% (2.4 gm)

NOTE: Original recipe contains approximately 300 calories and 15 grams of fat per serving.

Oven-Fried Onion Rings

Try this lower-fat version of a steak-house favorite with your favorite burger.

4 large yellow or sweet onions
1 cup all-purpose flour
1 cup nonalcoholic beer
1/4 teaspoon cayenne pepper (optional)
1/4 teaspoon salt or seasoning salt
1/4 teaspoon freshly ground pepper
2 egg whites, beaten to soft peaks
2 cups fine dry bread crumbs
1 1/2 to 2 tablespoons canola oil

Preheat the oven to 450 degrees. Cut the onions into 1/2-inch-thick slices and separate into rings; reserve the smallest inner rings for another recipe. In a large deep bowl, combine the flour, beer, cayenne, salt, and pepper, and whisk together. Gently fold in the egg whites; the batter should be light and fluffy. Spread the bread crumbs in a large shallow bowl.

Coat two 9 by 13-inch baking pans with 3/4 to 1 tablespoon canola oil each. Hook an onion ring on your finger and dip it into the batter, shaking off the excess; dip it into the bread crumbs and shake off the excess and place in one of the prepared baking pans. Repeat with the remaining onions and batter, placing the smaller rings inside the larger ones. (If you run out of room, you can layer them a little.) Bake for about 25 to 30 minutes, until lightly browned.

MAKES 4 TO 6 SERVINGS

Nutritional Analysis per Serving (6 servings per recipe):
Calories, 283; Fiber, 3.6 gm; Cholesterol, 2 mg; Sodium, 356 mg
% Calories from: Protein, 12%; Carbohydrate, 71%; Fat, 17%
(5 gm)

NOTE: Original recipe contains approximately 360 calories and
15 grams of fat per serving.

Red Beans and Rice

The original (fattier) version of this recipe appeared in the *Contra Costa Times* food section in the summer of 1995.

> 2 15¼-ounce cans (3 cups) kidney beans, drained and
>   rinsed
> ½ pound sliced lean ham, chopped
> 1¼ cups low-sodium chicken broth
> 1 cup chopped onions
> ¼ cup chopped green onions
> ¼ cup finely chopped green bell pepper
> 4 cloves garlic, minced
> 2 teaspoons dried parsley or 2 tablespoons minced
>   fresh parsley
> 2 bay leaves
> ½ teaspoon crushed dried basil
> ½ teaspoon dried thyme
> Freshly ground pepper to taste
> 3 slices Louis Rich less-fat turkey bacon, diced (optional)
> 4 cups cooked white rice

Place the beans, ham, broth, onions, green onions, green pepper, garlic, parsley, bay leaves, basil, thyme, pepper, and the turkey bacon, if using, in a large pot. Stir and bring to a boil. Reduce the heat to low and simmer for 45 minutes, stirring often.

Add the warmed rice and stir well.

MAKES 6 LARGE SERVINGS

Nutritional Analysis per Serving:
Calories, 356; Fiber, 2.3 gm; Cholesterol, 21 mg; Sodium, 942 mg
% Calories from: Protein, 23%; Carbohydrate, 69%; Fat, 8% (3 gm)

NOTE: Original recipe contains 634 calories, 90 milligrams cholesterol, and 17 grams of fat per serving.

Oysters Rockefeller

This is rich and delicious enough to serve at your most elegant dinner party. No one will ever guess you cut the fat of the original recipe almost in half!

1 tablespoon butter or margarine
½ 10-ounce package frozen chopped spinach, thawed
¼ cup nonalcoholic beer, white wine, or broth (chicken, beef, or vegetable)
¼ cup minced onion
1 tablespoon chopped fresh parsley
1 bay leaf, finely crumbled
¼ teaspoon salt
⅛ teaspoon cayenne pepper or ⅛ teaspoon hot pepper sauce
½ cup bread crumbs made from Oil-Free Croutons (page 68) or ¼ cup dried bread crumbs
18 large or 24 small oysters on the half-shell (have fishmonger open them)
3 slices Louis Rich less-fat turkey bacon, cooked until crisp and crumbled
3 tablespoons grated or shredded Parmesan cheese
Lemon wedges for garnish

Preheat the oven to 425 degrees. Melt the butter in a 1-quart saucepan over medium heat. Add the spinach, beer, onion, parsley, bay leaf, salt, and cayenne and cook, stirring occasionally, until the spinach is heated through. Stir in the bread crumbs and remove from the heat. Place the oysters in a baking pan and spoon on the spinach mixture. In a food processor, briefly blend the bacon pieces with the Parmesan cheese. Sprinkle the bacon mixture over the spinach mixture. Bake for 5 to 8 minutes, until lightly brown on top. Garnish with lemon wedges.
MAKES 9 SERVINGS

Nutritional Analysis per Serving:
Calories, 138; Fiber, 1 gm; Cholesterol, 60 mg; Sodium, 282 mg
% Calories from: Protein, 37%; Carbohydrate, 32%; Fat, 31%
(4.7 gm)

NOTE: Original recipe contains 173 calories, 69 milligrams cholesterol, and 8.3 grams of fat per serving.

Caesar Salad

Caesar salad may be the most popular salad served in restaurants. Among the many fat contributors to this salad are the croutons, so I created oil-free croutons. Another fat source—and potential salmonella source—is the raw egg in the dressing, so I used pasteurized fat-free egg substitute. But probably one of the biggest fat ingredients is the olive oil. I cut that way back and added reduced-fat mayonnaise and honey instead.

OIL-FREE CROUTONS
4 slices sourdough bread (or 8 slices baguette, cut into
*   3/4-inch cubes)*
Olive oil nonstick cooking spray
1 tablespoon shredded Parmesan cheese
1/2 teaspoon garlic powder
1/4 teaspoon freshly ground pepper

DRESSING
2 anchovy fillets
1 clove garlic, minced or pressed
1 tablespoon red wine vinegar
1 teaspoon Dijon mustard
3 1/2 tablespoons finely shredded Parmesan or Asiago cheese
1/4 teaspoon Worcestershire sauce
1 1/2 tablespoons fat-free egg substitute
1 tablespoon reduced-fat mayonnaise
1 tablespoon honey
2 tablespoons nonalcoholic beer or champagne
1 1/2 tablespoons olive oil
1 large head romaine lettuce, inner leaves only, torn into
*   bite-size pieces if desired*

Preheat the oven to 325 degrees. Place the bread cubes in a single layer on a cookie sheet. Spray the top of the bread with nonstick cooking spray. Flip the bread over and spray again.

In a small cup, blend the cheese, garlic powder, and pepper. Sprinkle over the bread. Bake for 5 to 10 minutes, or until the croutons are golden brown and crisp all the way through. Let cool.

In a blender or mini processor, combine the anchovies, garlic, vinegar, mustard, 1½ tablespoons of the Parmesan cheese, the Worcestershire sauce, egg substitute, mayonnaise, honey, and beer and blend until smooth. While the machine is running, add the oil in a steady stream and continue to blend until blended well.

Place the lettuce in a large bowl and toss with the dressing, croutons, and the remaining 2 tablespoons Parmesan cheese.
MAKES 4 SERVINGS

Nutritional Analysis per Serving:
Calories, 231; Fiber, 2.5 gm; Cholesterol, 10 mg; Sodium, 465 mg
% Calories from: Protein, 18%, Carbohydrate, 47%, Fat, 35% (9 gm)

NOTE: Original recipe contains 320 calories, 35 milligrams cholesterol, and 22 grams of fat per serving.

Classic Creamy Potato Salad

This light version of the summertime classic is perfect for a picnic or a buffet table.

½ cup Hellmann's/Best Foods light mayonnaise
¼ cup Hellmann's/Best Foods low-fat mayonnaise
¼ cup light sour cream
1 tablespoon desired vinegar—tarragon, white, or cider
1½ teaspoons Dijon mustard
½ teaspoon dried parsley flakes
¼ teaspoon dried thyme or 1 teaspoon finely chopped
    fresh thyme
2 teaspoons sugar
1 teaspoon salt
¼ teaspoon freshly ground pepper, or to taste
6 medium potatoes, peeled, cooked, and cubed (about
    5 cups)
1 cup sliced celery
½ cup chopped onions
2 hard-cooked egg whites, chopped

In a large bowl, combine the mayonnaises, sour cream, vinegar, mustard, parsley, thyme, sugar, salt, and pepper. Add the potatoes, celery, onions, and chopped egg whites. Toss to coat well. Cover and chill in the refrigerator until ready to serve.

MAKES 8 SERVINGS

Nutritional Analysis per Serving:

Calories, 243; Fiber, 4 gm; Cholesterol, 5 mg; Sodium, 503 mg
% Calories from: Protein, 8%; Carbohydrate, 72%; Fat, 20%
(5.5 gm)

NOTE: Original recipe contains 390 calories, 69 milligrams cholesterol, and 23 grams of fat per serving.

Creamy Macaroni Salad

My version of everybody's favorite macaroni salad has a third of the fat of the original recipe.

½ cup Hellmann's/Best Foods light mayonnaise
¼ cup Hellmann's/Best Foods low-fat mayonnaise
¼ cup light sour cream
2 tablespoons desired vinegar—white, cider, tarragon, or
   seasoned rice vinegar
1 tablespoon prepared mustard or Dijon
1½ teaspoons sugar
1 teaspoon salt
¼ teaspoon freshly ground pepper, or more to taste
8 ounces Mueller's elbow macaroni, cooked, drained, rinsed,
   and allowed to cool
1 cup sliced celery
1 cup chopped green or red bell peppers
⅓ cup chopped onion

In a large bowl, stir together the mayonnaises, sour cream, vinegar, mustard, sugar, salt, and peppers until smooth. Add the macaroni, celery, green peppers, and onion; toss to coat well. Cover and refrigerate for at least 2 hours to blend the flavors.

Just before serving, add more pepper to taste if necessary.
MAKES 10 SERVINGS

Nutritional Analysis per ½-Cup Serving:
Calories, 148; Fiber, 1.5 gm; Cholesterol, 5 mg; Sodium, 396 mg
% Calories from: Protein, 10%; Carbohydrate, 60%; Fat, 30%
(5 gm)

NOTE: Original recipe contains 253 calories, 13 milligrams cholesterol, and 18 grams of fat per ½-cup serving.

Onion-Roasted Potatoes

These potatoes make a delectable accompaniment to roast chicken, and they are *very* low in fat.

> 1 envelope Lipton Recipe Secrets onion or onion-mushroom
>   soup mix
> 1 tablespoon olive or vegetable oil
> 1 tablespoon honey
> 3 tablespoons apple juice or beer
> 2 pounds all-purpose potatoes, peeled and cut into large
>   chunks
> Chopped fresh parsley for garnish (optional)

Preheat the oven to 450 degrees. Place the soup mix in a large bowl. In a small saucepan, heat the oil, honey, and apple juice over medium heat, stirring frequently, for about 1 minute, or until blended and smooth. Add to the soup mix and stir to blend. Let cool for a few minutes, then add the potato chunks and toss with your hands to make sure all the potato pieces are well coated.

Coat a shallow baking or roasting pan with nonstick cooking spray. Spread the potatoes in a single layer in the pan. Bake, stirring occasionally, for 40 minutes, or until the potatoes are tender and golden brown. Garnish, if desired, with chopped parsley.

MAKES 8 SERVINGS

Nutritional Analysis per Serving:
Calories, 159; Fiber, 2 gm; Cholesterol, 0 mg; Sodium, 618 mg
% Calories from: Protein, 7%; Carbohydrate, 84%; Fat, 9%
(1.8 gm)

NOTE: Original recipe contains 212 calories and 9 grams of fat per serving.

Hot Artichoke Dip

Serve this at your next party. If you don't tell your guests you're using a "lightened-up" recipe, they'll never know the difference..

½ cup Hellman's/Best Foods reduced-fat mayonnaise
½ cup light sour cream
1 14-ounce jar artichoke hearts packed in water, drained and chopped
7 tablespoons grated Parmesan cheese
¼ teaspoon Tabasco
1 clove garlic, minced

Preheat the oven to 350 degrees. Combine all the ingredients in a large bowl and stir until well mixed. Spoon into a small baking dish. Bake for about 30 minutes, or until bubbly. Serve with re-duced-fat crackers or thinly sliced regular or sourdough baguette. MAKES 2 CUPS

Nutritional Analysis per ¼ Cup Dip:
Calories, 85; Fiber, 3 gm; Cholesterol, 17 mg; Sodium, 161 mg
% Calories from: Protein, 21%; Carbohydrate, 35%; Fat, 44%
(4 gm)

Nutritional Analysis per ¼ Cup Dip plus 1 Ounce SnackWell's Reduced-Fat Classic Golden Crackers:
Calories, 205; Fiber, 3 gm; Cholesterol, 17 mg; Sodium, 480 mg
% Calories from: Protein, 10%; Carbohydrate, 60%; Fat, 30%
(6.8 gm)

NOTE: Original recipe contains 197 calories, 18 milligrams choles-terol, and 19 grams of fat per ¼-cup serving of just the dip.

Honey-Roasted Party Mix

When the munchies strike, you can indulge your craving for something sweet and crunchy with this satisfying but lower-fat version of the famous Chex Party Mix.

2 tablespoons butter or margarine
1 teaspoon seasoned salt (or ¼ teaspoon garlic powder,
    ¼ teaspoon onion powder, and ¼ teaspoon salt)
2 tablespoons honey
1½ tablespoons Worcestershire sauce
8 cups of your favorite Chex brand cereals (corn, rice,
    and/or wheat)
1½ cups less-salt pretzel sticks
½ cup lightly salted mixed nuts or cashews

Preheat the oven to 250 degrees. Put the butter in a large roasting pan and melt in the oven. Stir in the seasoned salt, honey, and Worcestershire sauce. Gradually add the cereals, pretzels, and nuts, stirring until evenly coated.

Bake for 45 minutes to 1 hour, stirring every 15 minutes. Spread on paper towels to cool. Store in an airtight container or zip-top bags.

MAKES 9 CUPS

Nutritional Analysis per 1 Cup:
Calories, 210; Fiber, 2.5 gm; Cholesterol, 0 mg; Sodium, 400 mg
% Calories from: Protein, 8%; Carbohydrate, 63%, Fat, 29% (6.8 gm)

NOTE: Original recipe contains 259 calories and 14 grams of fat per cup.

Sour Cream–Onion Soup Dip

The reduced-fat or fat-free mayonnaise helps mellow the tang of the light sour cream in this light version of Lipton's classic back-of-the-box California Dip.

> *1 envelope Lipton Recipe Secrets onion soup mix*
> *1¾ cups light or fat-free sour cream*
> *¾ cup reduced-fat mayonnaise (or use ¼ cup real*
> *   mayonnaise and ½ cup fat-free)*

In a small bowl, blend the soup mix, sour cream, and mayonnaise. Chill until ready to serve. Serve with an assortment of raw vegetables such as zucchini, carrot, celery, and jícama sticks.
MAKES ABOUT 2½ CUPS

NOTE: The original recipe makes 2 cups of dip, but I found the dip to be a little too salty using only 2 cups of the light sour cream/reduced-fat mayonnaise mixture (the lower-fat sour cream brings out the saltiness).

Nutritional Analysis per ¼ Cup:
Calories, 89; Cholesterol, 23 mg; Sodium, 300 mg
% Calories from: Protein, 22%; Carbohydrate, 24%; Fat, 54% (5.5 gm)

NOTE: Original recipe contains 135 calories, 26 milligrams cholesterol, and 12 grams of fat per ¼ cup.

Sweet 'n' Sour Meatballs

Serve this lighter take on the venerable Heinz recipe to your family for dinner, over rice or fat-free noodles, or as finger food at a party.

1 pound ground sirloin or superlean ground beef
2 slices whole wheat bread, finely chopped, or 1 cup soft
    bread crumbs
1 egg
2 tablespoons minced onion
2 tablespoons 1% milk
2 cloves garlic, minced
1/2 teaspoon salt
Dash of freshly ground pepper
2 to 6 tablespoons nonalcoholic beer, beef broth, or water
    (optional)
1/2 cup Heinz chili sauce
1/2 cup red currant jelly

In a large bowl, combine the first 8 ingredients, mixing well with a wooden spoon or your hands. Form into 40 bite-size meatballs. Spray a nonstick frying pan with nonstick cooking spray and heat over medium-high heat. When the pan is hot, brown the meatballs. Cover and cook for 5 minutes. Turn the meatballs over, adding the beer if necessary to prevent sticking. Cover and simmer for an additional 5 minutes, or until the meatballs are cooked through.

Combine the chili sauce and jelly and pour over the meatballs. Simmer gently for about 10 minutes, stirring and basting the meatballs frequently until the sauce thickens nicely. Serve with toothpicks if desired.

MAKES 8 SERVINGS

Nutritional Analysis per Serving:
Calories, 182; Fiber, 1 gm; Cholesterol, 65 mg; Sodium, 448 mg
% Calories from: Protein, 33%; Carbohydrate, 45%; Fat, 22%
(4 gm)

NOTE: Original recipe contains 263 calories, 73 milligrams cholesterol, and 12 grams of fat per serving.

Spinach Dip

I've been to many a party where the table centerpiece—and main attraction—was a sourdough round carved into a bowl and filled with colorful spinach dip. If you hung around long enough, you could tear off pieces of the bread bowl (also known as "the best part"), which by the end of the evening would be nicely coated with the last remaining teaspoons of dip.

While lightening up this recipe, I added some garlic and another green onion to zip up the flavor, and some sugar to balance the tang of the light sour cream.

1 10-ounce package frozen chopped spinach, thawed and drained
2 cups light sour cream
½ cup Best Foods/Hellmann's light mayonnaise
½ cup Best Foods/Hellmann's low-fat mayonnaise
1 1.4-ounce package Knorr vegetable soup mix
1 8-ounce can water chestnuts, drained and chopped, or ¾ cup peeled and chopped jícama
4 green onions (white and light green parts), chopped
1 to 2 cloves garlic, minced or pressed
1 teaspoon sugar
1 large sourdough round (about 1½ pounds), carved into a bowl (optional; see first Note)

In a medium bowl, stir all the dip ingredients together well. Cover and chill for 2 hours.

Stir before serving. Serve the dip in the hollowed-out sourdough bread round if desired.

MAKES ABOUT 4 CUPS

NOTE: The bread you remove from the inside to make the "bowl" can be cut into cubes and served with the dip.

NOTE: The ingredients used here are, in my opinion, the best-tasting combination of lower-fat products, but you can, of course, use plain low-fat yogurt or nonfat sour cream instead of the light sour cream. You can also use all reduced-fat mayonnaise instead of half reduced-fat and half light mayonnaise.

Nutritional Analysis per ¼ Cup Dip:
Calories, 75; Fiber, 1.3 gm; Cholesterol, 6 mg; Sodium, 340 mg
% Calories from: Protein, 11%; Carbohydrate, 42%; Fat, 47%
(4 gm)

NOTE: Original recipe contains 180 calories, 21 milligrams cholesterol, and 17 grams of fat per ¼ cup dip.

Green Rice

Even kids have been known to eat this flavorful broccoli-rice casserole without complaint. Serve it as a side dish or a simple vegetarian supper.

> 1 10¾-ounce can Campbell's Healthy Request condensed cream of chicken soup, cream of mushroom soup, or cream of celery soup
> 1 cup 1% milk
> ⅔ cup light Cheez Whiz
> 2 10-ounce packages frozen chopped broccoli (spears can be used if you chop them up a little)
> 1½ cups instant rice
> ¼ cup minced onion
> ½ cup finely chopped celery
> 1 cup water chestnuts, drained and sliced

Preheat oven to 350 degrees. Spray a 9-inch square pan generously with nonstick cooking spray. In a large bowl, mix the soup and milk. Melt the Cheez Whiz in microwave or over medium heat and add to the soup mixture. Stir in all the remaining ingredients.

Pour the mixture into the prepared pan and bake for about 40 to 45 minutes, until bubbly.

MAKES 8 SERVINGS

Nutritional Analysis per Serving:
Calories, 195; Fiber, 3 gm; Cholesterol, 16 mg; Sodium, 412 mg
% Calories from: Protein, 17%; Carbohydrate, 56%; Fat, 27% (6 gm)

NOTE: Original recipe contains 244 calories, 31 milligrams cholesterol, and 14 grams of fat per serving.

Chapter 4

Breads and Brunches

Pumpkin Pecan Bread

You'll never miss the fat in this delicious variation of Libby's original recipe. Try it with a cup of coffee or tea as an afternoon snack.

2¾ cups all-purpose flour
1 tablespoon pumpkin pie spice
2 teaspoons baking powder
1 teaspoon baking soda
½ teaspoon salt
½ cup finely chopped pecans, plus ¼ cup (optional)
    pecan halves
¼ cup (½ stick) butter, softened
¼ cup fat-free cream cheese
½ cup light sour cream
1 cup granulated sugar
1 cup packed dark brown sugar
1 large egg
½ cup fat-free egg substitute
1 cup Libby's solid-pack pumpkin
1 teaspoon finely chopped orange zest
2 tablespoons Grand Marnier or other
    orange-flavored liqueur

Preheat the oven to 350 degrees. Coat two 8½ by 4½-inch loaf pans with nonstick cooking spray and lightly flour (or grease and flour the pans).

Combine the flour, pumpkin pie spice, baking powder, baking soda, salt, and pecans in a medium bowl.

In a large bowl, using an electric mixer, cream the butter, cream cheese, and sour cream. Add the sugars and beat until light. Add the egg and beat well, then add the egg substitute and beat well. Beat in the pumpkin, orange zest, and orange liqueur.

Add the dry ingredients to the pumpkin mixture and mix just until blended. Spoon into the prepared pans. Sprinkle pecan halves over the top if desired.

Bake for about 45 to 55 minutes, or until a wooden pick inserted in the center comes out clean. Cool for 10 minutes. Remove from the pans; cool completely on wire racks.

MAKES 20 SERVINGS (10 SLICES PER LOAF)

Nutritional Analysis per Serving:
Calories, 201; Fiber, 1 gm; Cholesterol, 17.5 mg; Sodium, 172 mg % Calories from: Protein, 7%; Carbohydrate, 72%; Fat, 21% (4.8 gm)

NOTE: Original recipe contains 279 calories, 67 milligrams cholesterol, and 14 grams of fat per serving.

Cheese Soufflé

Don't worry if your soufflé falls a little—it will still taste terrific!

2 tablespoons diet margarine
1¼ cups plus 5 tablespoons 1% milk
⅓ cup all-purpose flour
Dash of cayenne pepper
8 ounces reduced-fat sharp Cheddar cheese, grated
2 large egg yolks
2 tablespoons light or nonfat sour cream
6 large egg whites

Preheat the oven to 350 degrees. Coat a 2-quart soufflé dish with nonstick cooking spray. In a medium saucepan, melt the margarine with 5 tablespoons of the milk. Stir in the flour and cayenne pepper. Add the remaining 1¼ cups milk all at once and cook, stirring, until thickened and bubbly. Remove from the heat. Add half of the cheese, stirring until melted. Add the remaining cheese and stir until melted.

In a medium bowl, beat the egg yolks and sour cream with a fork until combined. Slowly add the cheese sauce to the yolks, stirring constantly. Let cool to room temperature.

In a large bowl, beat the egg whites until stiff peaks form. Fold half of the whites into the cheese sauce. Then fold the cheese sauce mixture into the remaining egg whites. Pour into the prepared soufflé dish. Bake for about 50 minutes, or until a knife inserted near the center comes out clean.

MAKES 6 SERVINGS

Nutritional Analysis per Serving:

Calories, 223; Fiber, 0.2 gm; Cholesterol, 94 mg; Sodium, 341 mg

% Calories from: Protein, 34%; Carbohydrate, 20%; Fat, 46% (11.5 gm)

NOTE: Original recipe contains 392 calories, 295 milligrams cholesterol, and 32 grams of fat per serving.

No-Cholesterol Crepes

These crepes are great whether filled with a sweet filling, such as strawberry jam, or a savory one, such as crab.

1 cup unbleached all-purpose flour
Pinch of salt
¼ cup fat-free egg substitute
1¼ cups 1% milk
2 egg whites

FOR SWEET CREPES (OPTIONAL)
2 tablespoons sugar and/or 2 teaspoons grated lemon zest
    and/or 1 teaspoon vanilla extract

Combine the flour and salt in a large bowl. In a small bowl, beat together the egg substitute and ½ cup of the milk. Stir into the flour mixture, then stir in the remaining ¾ cup milk. Beat thoroughly to incorporate air into the mixture.

In a medium bowl, beat the egg whites lightly until stiff. If making sweet crepes, add the sugar, lemon zest, and vanilla. Fold the egg whites gently into the batter.

Cover and let sit for 30 to 60 minutes. (You can make the batter the night before and refrigerate it until morning.)

Heat a medium nonstick frying or crepe pan until a drop of water dances on the surface. Coat generously with nonstick cooking spray. Pour in about 2 tablespoons of batter and tilt the pan to coat the bottom. Cook until set, then loosen the edge and flip the crepe over with a spatula. Cook for about 20 seconds longer, until bottom is set or lightly browned, depending on how you like your crepes. Repeat with the remaining batter. It's okay to stack the crepes before filling them.

MAKES ABOUT 18 CREPES

Nutritional Analysis per 2 Crepes:
Calories, 76; Fiber, 0.4 gm; Cholesterol, 2.5 mg; Sodium, 66 mg
% Calories from: Protein, 22%; Carbohydrate, 68%; Fat, 10%
(0.8 gm)

NOTE: Original recipe contains 122 calories, 62 milligrams cholesterol, and 6 grams of fat per 2 crepes.

Belgian Waffles

I've been to Belgium and you'd better believe I've had the waffles. They were a bit sweeter and fluffier than our waffles. I had to invent my own low-fat Belgian waffle recipe, since I could not find an original to lighten up. You can use a Belgian waffle iron or a regular one.

2 cups all-purpose flour
1 tablespoon baking powder
1/2 teaspoon salt
2 egg yolks
1 1/2 cups 1% milk
2 tablespoons butter, melted
1 1/2 teaspoons vanilla extract
3 egg whites
6 tablespoons sugar

Combine the flour, baking powder, and salt in a medium bowl. In a large bowl, beat in the egg yolks well. Stir in the milk, butter, and vanilla. Add the flour mixture and beat until smooth.

In a medium bowl, beat the egg whites until stiff but not dry. Slowly add the sugar, beating constantly. Gently stir one third of the egg whites into the batter. Carefully fold in another third, then fold in the remaining whites.

Heat a waffle iron and coat with nonstick cooking spray. Pour 1/2 cup of the batter into the waffle iron (or follow the instructions for your waffle iron). Bake until golden. Repeat with the remaining batter. Serve immediately.

MAKES ABOUT 6 STANDARD-SIZE WAFFLES

Nutritional Analysis per Waffle:
Calories, 290; Fiber, 1 gm; Cholesterol, 83 mg; Sodium, 443 mg
% Calories from: Protein, 13%; Carbohydrate, 67%; Fat, 20%
(6.5 gm)

NOTE: Original recipe contains 345 calories, 135 milligrams cholesterol, and 13 grams of fat per waffle.

Quick Focaccia

This quick bread has an authentic Italian flavor and is no more difficult to make than a batch of biscuits!

2 tablespoons olive oil
2 garlic cloves, minced or pressed
Olive oil nonstick cooking spray
3 cups Bisquick reduced-fat baking mix
2 teaspoons rubbed sage or 1 teaspoon ground sage
1 cup 1% milk
⅓ cup shredded Parmesan cheese
¾ teaspoon dried oregano leaves
¼ to ½ teaspoon salt

Combine the oil and garlic in a small cup and set aside. (If possible, allow the oil to steep overnight before using.)

Preheat the oven to 400 degrees. Coat a 13 by 9-inch baking pan generously with olive oil nonstick cooking spray. In a large bowl, blend the baking mix with the sage. Stir in the milk until well mixed. Turn the biscuit dough into the prepared pan and pat out evenly with floured fingertips. Make indentations in the dough with your fingertips at 1-inch intervals.

Spread the garlic-oil mixture evenly over the dough with your fingertips. In a small bowl, stir the Parmesan cheese, oregano, and salt together. (Or combine in a mini food processor.) Sprinkle the dough with the cheese mixture.

Bake for 25 minutes, or until nicely browned on top. Cut into rectangles and serve warm.

Makes 8 servings

Nutritional Analysis per Serving:

Calories, 230; Fiber, 1 gm; Cholesterol, 4.5 mg; Sodium, 700 mg
% Calories from: Protein, 12%; Carbohydrate, 57%; Fat, 31%
(7.8 gm)

NOTE: Original recipe contains 300 calories and 18 grams of fat
per serving.

Yeast Focaccia with Tomato and Cheese

Served with soup and a green salad, this pizzalike bread makes a light meal.

2 tablespoons extra-virgin olive oil
2 cloves garlic, minced or pressed

DOUGH:
1¾ cups warm water (110° to 115°)
1 tablespoon sugar
1 package (1 tablespoon) rapid-rise yeast
5 cups unbleached all-purpose flour
2 tablespoons extra-virgin olive oil
1 teaspoon salt

Olive oil nonstick cooking spray
⅓ cup shredded Parmesan cheese
¾ teaspoon dried oregano
¼ to ½ teaspoon salt
⅔ cup low-fat bottled spaghetti sauce or tomato sauce
4 ounces part-skim or low-fat mozzarella cheese, grated

Combine the oil and garlic in a small cup and set aside. (If possible, allow the oil to steep overnight before using.)

In a medium bowl, combine the water, sugar, and yeast and gently stir until the yeast is dissolved. Let stand 5 minutes, or until foamy. Stir in 1 cup of the flour, then stir in the oil and salt. Stir in the remaining 4 cups flour. Knead briefly on a floured surface to incorporate the flour.

Let the dough rest while you preheat the oven to 450 degrees. Generously coat a 13 by 9-inch baking pan with olive oil nonstick cooking spray.

Turn the dough into the pan and pat out evenly with your

fingertips. Flour your fingertips and make indentations in the surface of the dough at 1-inch intervals.

Spread the garlic-oil mixture evenly over the dough with your fingertips.

In a small bowl, stir together the Parmesan cheese, oregano, and salt. (Or combine in a mini food processor.) Sprinkle the dough with the cheese mixture.

Bake for 15 to 20 minutes, or until the top is nicely browned. Turn the oven off. Spread the spaghetti sauce evenly over the focaccia. Top with the mozzarella and put back in the warm oven until the cheese is melted. Cut into rectangles and serve warm.
MAKES 12 SERVINGS

Nutritional Analysis per Serving:
Calories, 276; Fiber, 1.6 gm; Cholesterol, 7 mg; Sodium, 428 mg
% Calories from: Protein, 14%; Carbohydrate, 62%; Fat, 25%
(7 gm)

NOTE: Original recipe contains 333 calories and 14 grams of fat per serving

Fancy Department Store Blueberry Muffins

These cake-like muffins are good enough for dessert, or make them for Sunday breakfast for a real treat.

2 cups King Arthur unbleached all-purpose flour
1 tablespoon baking powder
¼ teaspoon salt
3 tablespoons butter or margarine, softened
3 tablespoons fat-free cream cheese
1¼ cups sugar
1 egg
2 tablespoons fat-free egg substitute
1 teaspoon vanilla extract
½ cup low-fat buttermilk
1 15-ounce can Wild Maine blueberries, drained, or 2 cups
fresh or frozen (unthawed) blueberries
Spiced sugar (3 tablespoons sugar mixed with ¾ teaspoon
ground cinnamon (optional)

Preheat the oven to 400 degrees. Coat nonstick regular or extra-large muffin cups generously with nonstick cooking spray, or use foil muffin cups. In a medium bowl, combine the flour, baking powder, and salt. Set aside. In a large bowl, with an electric mixer, cream the butter or margarine, cream cheese, and sugar until light and fluffy. Add the egg, egg substitute, and vanilla and beat well. Beat in the dry ingredients alternately with the buttermilk. Gently fold in the blueberries.

Fill each regular-size muffin cup with a slightly heaping ¼ cup of batter or fill each extra-large muffin cup with ½ cup of batter. Sprinkle the tops with spiced sugar if desired. Bake for 20 to 30 minutes, or until golden brown on top.

MAKES 12 REGULAR-SIZE MUFFINS OR 7 EXTRA-LARGE MUFFINS

Nutritional Analysis per Regular-Size Muffin:
Calories, 208; Fiber, 1 gm; Cholesterol, 25 mg; Sodium, 178 mg
% Calories from: Protein, 7%; Carbohydrate, 78%; Fat, 16%
(3.5 gm)

NOTE: Original recipe contains 250 calories, and 52 milligrams
cholesterol, and 7.5 grams fat per regular-size muffin.

Quiche Lorraine

Once upon a time we were all quiche-crazy. Now you can enjoy this rich-tasting but lower-fat version for brunch or a light supper and not worry about your fat grams.

1 small onion, sliced into ¼-inch rings
¼ cup beer
8 slices Louis Rich less-fat turkey bacon
1 unbaked 9-inch Light and Flaky Piecrust (page 223)
        or 1 Biscuit Crust (recipe follows)
2 large eggs
½ cup fat-free egg substitute
1 cup 1% milk
½ teaspoon freshly grated nutmeg or ⅛ teaspoon
        ground nutmeg
½ teaspoon salt
4 ounces reduced-fat Swiss cheese or part-skim Jarlsberg,
        grated (1 cup firmly packed)

Preheat the oven to 425 degrees. Coat a nonstick frying pan generously with nonstick cooking spray. Sauté the onion rings over medium heat until lightly browned. Gently flip the rings over, let brown on the other side, add the beer, and cook until most of the beer has evaporated. Set aside.

In a large frying pan, cook the turkey bacon over low heat until crisp and brown. Drain the bacon on paper towels and crumble. Spread the crumbled bacon in the prepared piecrust.

In a medium bowl, with a wire whisk, beat the eggs, egg substitute, milk, nutmeg, and salt. Stir in the cheese. Pour the egg mixture into the crust.

Bake for 15 minutes. Turn oven control to 325 degrees. Arrange the onion rings decoratively on top of the partially cooked quiche. Return to the oven and bake for about 30 minutes longer, or until a knife inserted in the center comes out clean. Let stand for 10 minutes before serving.

MAKES 8 SERVINGS

Nutritional Analysis per Serving (made with Light and Flaky Piecrust):
Calories, 269; Fiber, 1 gm; Cholesterol, 76 mg; Sodium, 589 mg
% Calories from: Protein, 20%; Carbohydrate, 30%; Fat, 50%
(15 gm)

NOTE: Original recipe contains 380 calories, 155 milligrams cholesterol, and 30 grams of fat per serving.

Nutritional Analysis per Serving (made with Biscuit Crust):
Calories, 184; Fiber, 1 gm; Cholesterol, 75 mg; Sodium, 629 mg
% Calories from: Protein, 25%; Carbohydrate, 35%; Fat, 40%
(8 gm)

Biscuit Crust

1 cup Bisquick reduced-fat baking mix
3 tablespoons low-fat buttermilk
3 tablespoons 1% milk

In a small bowl, blend the Bisquick with the buttermilk and milk. Turn out onto a lightly floured cutting board and knead until smooth. Roll out with a rolling pin into an 11-inch round. Press into a 9-inch pie pan.

Extra-Sticky Sticky Buns

My husband has one motto about sticky buns, and that is that you can never use too much sticky glaze to make a sticky bun. So I added 50 percent more brown sugar glaze to coat the pan with the pecans. The result? Extra-wonderful, extra-sticky sticky buns.

1 package (1 tablespoon) quick-rise yeast
1/3 cup sugar
1 teaspoon salt
1/2 teaspoon ground cardamom (optional)
*About 3 3/4 cups all-purpose flour (or use 1 1/2 cups whole
    wheat flour and about 2 1/4 cups all-purpose flour)*
3/4 cup plus 2 tablespoons 1% milk
1/4 cup (1/2 stick) butter
2 tablespoons light sour cream
1 large egg
2 tablespoons fat-free egg substitute
3/4 cup raisins
2 tablespoons maple syrup
1/3 cup plus 1/2 cup packed dark brown sugar
1 cup pecan halves
1/4 cup apple juice
3/4 teaspoon ground cinnamon

ICING (OPTIONAL)
1/3 cup confectioners' sugar
1 teaspoon water

In a large bowl, combine the yeast, sugar, and salt. Add the cardamom if using and 1 1/2 cups flour. In a small saucepan over low heat, heat the milk and 1 tablespoon of the butter until very warm (125 to 130 degrees); the butter does not need to melt completely. Remove from the heat and stir in the sour cream.

With an electric mixer on low speed, gradually beat the warm liquid milk mixture, egg, and egg substitute into the dry ingredients just until blended, scraping the bowl often with a rubber spatula. Increase the speed to medium and beat for 3 minutes. With a wooden spoon, stir in 2 cups flour to make a soft dough.

Turn dough out onto a floured surface and knead until smooth and elastic, about 10 minutes, working in up to ¼ cup more flour until the dough is no longer sticky. Shape the dough into a ball; cover and let rest 15 minutes.

Meanwhile, in a small saucepan over low heat, melt 1 tablespoon of the butter. Stir in the raisins, maple syrup, and ⅓ cup brown sugar.

Generously spray a 9½-inch tube pan with a removable bottom and a 5 by 8½-inch loaf pan with nonstick cooking spray. Spread the pecan halves evenly in the pans. In a small saucepan, bring the remaining ½ cup brown sugar, remaining 2 tablespoons butter, and the apple juice to a low boil over medium heat, stirring constantly until smooth. Stir in the cinnamon. Pour over the pecans in the pans.

On a lightly floured surface, with a floured rolling pin, roll the dough in a rectangle about 18 by 12 inches. Spread the butter-raisin mixture over the dough, leaving a ½-inch border. Starting from a long side, roll up the dough jelly-roll fashion. With a serrated knife, slice the roll crosswise into 10 pieces. Set the pieces swirl side up in the prepared pans, 7 in the tube pan and 3 in the loaf pan Cover the pans loosely and let the rolls rise in a warm place until doubled in size, about 30 minutes.

Preheat the oven to 350 degrees. Uncover the rolls and bake for about 25 minutes, or until golden brown on top. Let cool in the pan for 10 minutes.

Lift the center of the tube pan up to separate it from the sides. Loosen the rolls from the pan with a knife. Turn the tube upside down and flip the rolls, pecan side up, onto a serving plate. Loosen the rolls from the sides of the loaf pan with a knife and invert onto a serving plate.

While the rolls are baking, make the icing, if desired: Combine the confectioners' sugar and water in a small bowl and mix until smooth, adding a few drops more water if necessary. Drizzle the icing over the rolls.

MAKES 10 LARGE ROLLS

Nutritional Analysis per Roll (without icing):
Calories, 445; Fiber, 2.6 gm; Cholesterol, 35 mg; Sodium, 293 mg
% Calories from: Protein, 7%; Carbohydrate, 67%; Fat, 26%
(13 gm)

NOTE: Original recipe (made with less brown sugar glaze) contains 500 calories, 35 milligrams cholesterol, and 26 grams of fat per roll.

Flaky Baking Powder Biscuits

Light and flaky, the perfect finishing touch to any meal.

2 cups sifted all-purpose flour
1 tablespoon baking powder
1½ teaspoons sugar
1 teaspoon salt
3 tablespoons butter-flavor Crisco
2 tablespoons fat-free cream cheese
⅓ cup low-fat buttermilk
6 to 7 tablespoons 1% milk

Preheat the oven to 350 degrees. In a medium bowl, mix the flour, baking powder, sugar, and salt. With a pastry blender, two knives, or a fork, cut in the Crisco and cream cheese until mixture looks like coarse meal. Add the buttermilk and 6 tablespoons of the milk and stir just until the dough comes together, adding another tablespoon of milk if necessary. Place on a lightly floured surface and knead lightly. Roll the dough out ½ inch thick. Cut out biscuits with a 2-inch floured biscuit cutter and place 1 inch apart on an ungreased cookie sheet. Bake for 12 to 15 minutes, until golden brown.

MAKES 16 SMALL BISCUITS

Nutritional Analysis per Biscuit:
Calories, 85; Fiber 0.5 gm; Cholesterol, 0.4 mg; Sodium, 203 mg
% Calories from: Protein, 9%; Carbohydrate, 62%; Fat, 28% (2.7 gm)

NOTE: Original recipe contains 101 calories and 4.5 grams of fat per biscuit.

CHEESE BISCUITS: Add ½ cup shredded reduced-fat sharp Cheddar before stirring in the buttermilk.

Cheesy Brunch Casserole

This brunch classic is full of cheese flavor and good-for-you veggies, but it has less than half the fat and calories of the original recipe. I like to serve this dish with mild salsa on top.

12 cups ½-inch cubes of bread (1 regular loaf white or whole wheat; I also like to use sourdough or French bread)
12 ounces Kraft reduced-fat sharp Cheddar cheese, shredded (3 cups)
3 cups sliced zucchini or 2 cups broccoli flowerets
1 green or red bell pepper, chopped
6 green onions (white and light green parts), chopped
4 large eggs
1 cup fat-free egg substitute
2½ cups 1% milk
½ cup light or nonfat sour cream

Preheat the oven to 350 degrees. Coat a 13 by 9-inch baking dish generously with nonstick cooking spray. Layer half the bread and then half the cheese in the pan. Top with half the vegetables. Repeat the layers with the remaining bread, cheese, and vegetables.

In a large bowl, beat the eggs and egg substitute. Add the milk and sour cream, beating until smooth. Pour evenly over the casserole. Bake for 50 minutes to 1 hour, or until golden brown on top and custard is set.

MAKES 8 LARGE SERVINGS

You can cut all the ingredients in half and assemble in a 9-inch square baking dish. Bake for 40 to 45 minutes, or until lightly brown on top and custard is set.

MAKES 4 LARGE SERVINGS

Nutritional Analysis per Serving:
Calories, 371; Fiber, 2 gm; Cholesterol, 133 mg; Sodium, 676 mg
% Calories from: Protein, 29%; Carbohydrate, 42%; Fat, 30%
(12 gm)

NOTE: Original recipe contains 628 calories, 286 milligrams cholesterol, and 40 grams of fat per serving.

Eggs Benedict

The fat and calorie counts of the original recipe were off the charts. This dish is still an indulgence, but not one you have to swear off forever.

4 large eggs
4 English muffins, split
8 slices Canadian bacon or lean cooked ham (cut to
*   fit muffins)*
1 cup Light Hollandaise Sauce (recipe follows), warm

Poach the eggs until desired doneness (or fry in a nonstick frying pan, coated generously with nonstick cooking spray, to desired doneness). Keep warm.

Preheat the broiler. Place the muffin halves on the broiler pan and broil until lightly toasted. Broil the Canadian bacon alongside the muffin halves (or panfry in a nonstick frying pan, coated with nonstick cooking spray, for about a minute on each side).

Place 2 muffin halves, side by side, on each plate. Put a slice of Canadian bacon on each muffin half. Top each serving with 1 cooked egg (or cut each egg in half and top each muffin half with an egg half). Generously spoon the Hollandaise Sauce over the eggs.

MAKES 4 SERVINGS

Nutritional Analysis per Serving (with ¼ cup sauce):
Calories, 415; Fiber, 1.5 gm; Cholesterol, 386 mg; Sodium, 1360 mg
% Calories from: Protein, 27%; Carbohydrate, 30%; Fat, 43% (19 gm)

NOTE: Original recipe contains 872 calories, 893 milligrams cholesterol, and 69 grams of fat per serving of 2 English muffin halves topped with 2 eggs, 2 slices Canadian bacon, and 1/4 cup sauce.

Light Hollandaise Sauce

3 large egg yolks
6 tablespoons fat-free egg substitute
4 to 5 tablespoons lemon juice (to taste)
2½ tablespoons butter
⅓ cup light sour cream
1 tablespoon cornstarch
⅓ cup milk
½ teaspoon salt

Place the egg yolks, egg substitute, and lemon juice in the top of a double broiler. Beat with a wire whisk until smooth. Place over hot but not boiling water and set over low heat. Add the butter to the egg yolk mixture and whisk until completely melted. Mix the sour cream with the cornstarch and whisk into the egg yolk mixture until blended. Add the milk, whisking constantly, and cook, whisking, until the mixture thickens and is heated through. Remove from the heat and stir in the salt. Keep warm over low heat.

MAKES 1⅓ CUPS

Chapter 5

Entrées

Italian Hero Sandwiches

One of the problems with an Italian Hero Sandwich—fat-wise anyway—is the sheer weight of sausage used to fill one sandwich (three links!). In order to make a lower-fat sandwich, not only do you need to use a reduced-fat sweet Italian sausage (usually a turkey product), but you need to use only one link for each roll. Fortunately there are plenty of sautéed vegetables to help flavor the sandwiches. And splitting the sausages lengthwise in order to cover the bread gives the impression that there is plenty of meat in these sandwiches.

Olive oil nonstick cooking spray
4 links (3 ounces each) sweet lean Italian turkey sausage
    (such as The Turkey Store brand, 10% fat)
1/3 to 2/3 cup nonalcoholic beer, light beer, or water
1 tablespoon olive oil
2 medium onions, thinly sliced
4 green or red bell peppers, cut into 1/2-inch strips
4 5-inch-long hard rolls

Heat a medium nonstick skillet over medium heat. Coat the pan generously with olive oil nonstick cooking spray. Add the sausages and 1/3 cup of the beer, reduce the heat to low, and cover the pan. Simmer for about 6 minutes. Remove the cover and continue cooking for about 15 minutes longer, or until the sausages are browned and no longer pink in the center; add an additional 1/3 cup beer if needed to prevent sticking.

While the sausages are cooking, heat the olive oil in a large nonstick skillet over medium-low heat. Add the onions and peppers and cook, stirring occasionally, until the peppers are tender, about 10 minutes; after the first 5 minutes, add up to 1 1/2 cups water to the pan as needed to help cook the vegetables.

Preheat the broiler. Split the rolls lengthwise in half. Spray the split sides with olive oil nonstick spray if desired. Set under the broiler briefly just to crisp the bread.

Cut the sausages lengthwise in half. Layer the pepper and onion mixture and the split links on the roll bottoms. Add the tops of the rolls. Cut each roll crosswise in half for easier eating.

MAKES 4 SERVINGS

Nutritional Analysis per Serving:
Calories, 376; Fiber, 3.3 gm; Cholesterol, 46 mg; Sodium, 866 mg
% Calories from: Protein, 20%; Carbohydrate, 46%; Fat, 34% (14 gm)

NOTE: Original recipe contains 914 calories and 60 grams of fat per serving.

Poor Boy Sandwiches with Russian Dressing

There are many variations on this popular sandwich, which goes by a number of different names in different parts of the country. This is a lighter version of a classic hero sandwich.

Half of 1 1-pound loaf unsliced French bread
3 tablespoons Russian Dressing (recipe follows)
2 tablespoons chopped green onion
½ cucumber, sliced
6 ounces sliced premium very lean ham
4 ounces sliced reduced-fat Swiss cheese or light Jarlsberg
1 tomato, sliced

With a sharp knife, cut the bread horizontally in half. In a small bowl, mix the Russian dressing with the chopped green onion. On the bottom of the bread, layer the cucumber slices, ham, cheese, and tomato. Spread the Russian dressing generously on top. Replace the top of bread. Slice into equal pieces to serve.
MAKES 3 SERVINGS

Nutritional Analysis per Serving (including 1 tablespoon Russian dressing):

Calories, 405; Fiber, 2.3 gm; Cholesterol, 47 mg; Sodium, 1530 mg
% Calories from: Protein, 28%; Carbohydrate, 48%; Fat, 24% (10.8 gm)

NOTE: Original recipe contains 637 calories, 151 milligrams cholesterol, and 35 grams of fat per serving.

Russian Dressing

2 tablespoons low-fat, light, or fat-free mayonnaise
2 tablespoons catsup
¼ teaspoon hot sauce or chili sauce
1 teaspoon sugar
1½ teaspoons seasoned rice vinegar, white wine vinegar, or
    distilled white vinegar
1 teaspoon lemon juice
¼ teaspoon Worcestershire sauce
⅛ teaspoon salt
Pinch or two of freshly ground pepper

Combine all the ingredients in a small bowl; stir well to blend. The dressing can be stored, covered, in the refrigerator for up to 2 weeks; stir before serving.

MAKES 5 TABLESPOONS

Nutritional Analysis per 1 Tablespoon (Poor Boy Nutritional Analysis includes this dressing):
Calories, 18; Cholesterol, 3 mg; Sodium, 131 mg
% Calories from: Protein, 3%; Carbohydrate, 61%; Fat, 36% (0.8 gm)

Crispy Oven-Fried Chicken

This is the closest I've come to the distinctive Kentucky Fried Chicken flavor, without all the fat that comes from deep-frying. If you want it to taste even more like KFC Chicken, add a teaspoon of MSG (Accent or any other brand) to the flour mixture.

1 tablespoon butter flavor shortening
¼ cup 1% milk
1 large egg
1 cup all-purpose flour
1 teaspoon garlic powder
1 teaspoon paprika
½ teaspoon poultry seasoning
1 teaspoon salt
¾ teaspoon freshly ground pepper
6 skinless chicken breast halves (see Note)
Vegetable-oil nonstick cooking spray

Preheat the oven to 350 degrees. Line a 9 by 13-inch baking pan with foil and grease the foil with 1½ teaspoons of the shortening. Blend the milk and egg in a medium bowl. Combine the flour, garlic powder, paprika, poultry seasoning, salt, and pepper in a plastic bag or a medium bowl. Shake or toss the chicken in the flour mixture to coat. Dip the chicken pieces into the egg mixture, then shake or toss a second time in the flour mixture to coat well.

Place the chicken in the prepared baking pan. Generously spray the chicken with nonstick cooking spray. Melt the remaining 1½ teaspoons shortening and drizzle evenly over the chicken.

Bake for about 30 minutes. Turn the chicken over and bake for an additional 15 to 20 minutes, or until browned on both sides and cooked through. Let cool, then cover well and refrigerate.
MAKES 6 SERVINGS

NOTE: You can use boneless, skinless chicken breasts if desired; the recipe makes enough to coat 8 boneless breasts.

Nutritional Analysis per Serving:

Calories, 258; Fiber, 0.6 gm; Cholesterol, 110 mg; Sodium, 352 mg
% Calories from: Protein, 49%; Carbohydrate, 27%; Fat, 24% (6.6 gm)

NOTE: One Original Recipe Kentucky Fried Chicken breast contains 260 calories and 14 grams of fat.

Simple Salisbury Steak

By using ground sirloin instead of chuck, lower-fat cream of mushroom soup rather than regular, and egg substitute instead of whole eggs, I cut the fat and calories of this time-honored recipe by half.

> 1 10¾-ounce can Campbell's Healthy Request condensed
>   cream of mushroom soup
> 1 pound ground sirloin
> ⅓ cup dry bread crumbs
> ¼ cup fat-free egg substitute
> ½ cup finely chopped onions
> ¼ cup nonalcoholic beer, beef broth, or water (optional)
> 1½ cups (about 4 ounces) sliced mushrooms

In a large bowl, mix ¼ cup of the condensed soup, the ground sirloin, bread crumbs, egg substitute, and ¼ cup of the onions. Shape firmly into 6 oval patties, about ½ inch thick.

Coat a large nonstick skillet with nonstick cooking spray. Cook the patties over medium heat, turning once for 10 to 12 minutes, or until browned on both sides; add the beer if necessary to prevent sticking. Remove the patties from the pan and set aside.

Add the mushrooms and the remaining soup and onions to the pan and heat to boiling. Return the patties to the pan, reduce the heat to low, cover, and cook for 10 minutes, or until the patties are cooked through, stirring occasionally.

MAKES 6 SERVINGS

Nutritional Analysis per Serving:

Calories, 173; Fiber, 1 gm; Cholesterol, 41 mg; Sodium, 297 mg
% Calories from: Protein, 43%; Carbohydrate, 24%; Fat, 33% (6 gm)

NOTE: Original recipe contains 278 calories, 86 milligrams cholesterol, and 19 grams of fat per serving.

Quick Macaroni and Cheese

You can serve this rich-tasting version of a classic favorite to your family without feeling guilty.

> 1 cup 1% milk (or similar)
> 2½ tablespoons Gold Medal Wondra flour
>   (quick-mixing flour)
> ¼ teaspoon garlic powder
> ¼ teaspoon dry mustard
> ⅛ teaspoon seasoning salt or salt
> ⅛ teaspoon freshly ground pepper
> 4 ounces reduced-fat sharp Cheddar cheese, shredded
> 4 cups cooked macaroni (about 2 cups, or 6 ounces, dry)

In a medium nonstick saucepan, combine the milk, flour, garlic powder, mustard, seasoning salt, and pepper and bring to a boil over medium heat, stirring constantly. Boil, stirring, for about 1 minute, or until thickened. Stir in the cheese and stir until melted. Add the macaroni and stir to blend.
MAKES 4 SERVINGS

Nutritional Analysis per Serving:
Calories, 320; Fiber, 2.4 gm; Cholesterol, 18 mg; Sodium, 246 mg % Calories from: Protein, 22%; Carbohydrate, 60%; Fat, 18% (6 gm)

NOTE: Original recipe contains 413 calories, 54 milligrams cholesterol, and 18 grams of fat per serving.

Fettuccine Alfredo

Fettuccine Alfredo should be creamy and rich. I found that if I cut the butter by two-thirds and used whole milk instead of heavy cream but used the same amount of Parmesan cheese, I had a creamy, rich, and wonderful version of fettuccine Alfredo that has less than one-fourth the fat of the original.

2 tablespoons butter
1½ cups whole milk
4 cups hot cooked fettuccine (about 4 cups dry, or 8 ounces)
1 cup grated Parmesan cheese
Freshly grated nutmeg to taste (or about ⅛ teaspoon ground nutmeg)
Salt and freshly ground pepper to taste
4 strips Louis Rich less-fat turkey bacon, cooked until crisp and crumbled (optional)

In a large nonstick frying pan, melt the butter over medium heat and cook until lightly browned. Add ½ cup of the milk and boil rapidly, stirring occasionally, until large, shiny bubbles form. Reduce the heat to medium-low, add the noodles, and toss vigorously with two forks. Add the cheese and then gradually add the remaining 1 cup milk, in about 3 additions. Season generously with nutmeg and with salt and pepper. Sprinkle the crumbled bacon over the top, if using.

MAKES 4 GENEROUS SERVINGS

Nutritional Analysis per Serving:
Calories, 367; Fiber, 2.2 gm; Cholesterol, 37 mg; Sodium, 402 mg
% Calories from: Protein, 18%; Carbohydrate, 49%; Fat, 33% (13 gm)

NOTE: Original recipe contains approximately 800 calories, 179 milligrams cholesterol, and 58 grams of fat per serving.

Cajun Meat Loaf

This lighter version of chef Paul Prudhomme's spicy meat loaf packs its punch in taste, not fat and calories.

SEASONING MIX
2 bay leaves
1 teaspoon salt (optional)
1/2 to 1 teaspoon cayenne pepper
1/2 to 1 teaspoon freshly ground pepper
1/4 to 1/2 teaspoon white pepper
1/2 teaspoon ground cumin
1/2 teaspoon ground or grated nutmeg

1 tablespoon butter
1/4 cup nonalcoholic beer
3/4 cup finely chopped onions
1/2 cup finely chopped celery
1/2 cup finely chopped green bell peppers
1/4 cup finely chopped green onions
4 cloves garlic, minced or pressed
1 tablespoon Tabasco
2 to 3 teaspoons Worcestershire sauce
1/2 cup evaporated skimmed milk
1/2 cup catsup
1 1/2 pounds ground sirloin
1/2 pound pork tenderloin (or lean boneless pork chops),
    trimmed of any visible fat and ground in a food
    processor
1/2 cup fat-free egg substitute
1 cup very fine dry bread crumbs

Combine the seasoning mix ingredients in a small bowl and set aside. Melt the butter in a large nonstick saucepan over medium-low heat. Add the beer, onions, celery, bell peppers, green onions, garlic, Tabasco, Worcestershire, and seasoning mix and sauté until the mixture starts sticking to the bottom of the pan, about 6 minutes, stirring frequently. Stir in the milk and catsup and simmer for 2 minutes, stirring occasionally. Remove from the heat and let cool to room temperature.

Preheat the oven to 350 degrees. Coat two 9 by 9-inch loaf pans or a 6 by 12-inch baking pan with nonstick cooking spray. Place the beef and pork in a large bowl and add the egg substitute, cooked vegetable mixture (remove the bay leaves), and bread crumbs. Mix with your hands to thoroughly combine. Divide in half and shape into loaves in the two prepared loaf pans or place in the baking pan.

Bake uncovered for 25 minutes. Increase the oven temperature to 400 degrees and cook until a cut slice looks done, about 25 to 30 minutes more.

MAKES 8 SERVINGS

Nutritional Analysis per Serving:
Calories, 296; Fiber, 1.3 gm; Cholesterol, 84 mg; Sodium, 695 mg
% Calories from: Protein, 43%; Carbohydrate, 25%; Fat, 32%
(10 gm)

NOTE: Original recipe contains 470 calories, 150 milligrams cholesterol, and 34 grams of fat per serving.

Prize-Winning Meat Loaf

Delicious hot for dinner or cold and sliced in a sandwich.

1 cup V8 Picante (vegetable juice) or tomato juice
¾ cup quick or old-fashioned Quaker Oats
¼ cup fat-free egg substitute
½ cup chopped onions
½ teaspoon salt
½ teaspoon freshly ground pepper
2 garlic cloves, minced or pressed
1 teaspoon dried oregano
1½ pounds ground sirloin (or the leanest ground beef you
*   can get your hand on) (see Note)*

Preheat the oven to 350 degrees. Generously coat an 8 by 4-inch loaf pan with nonstick cooking spray. Combine all the ingredients except the ground beef in a large bowl and mix well with your hands. Add the ground beef and mix thoroughly. Shape into a loaf in the prepared pan.

Bake for 1 hour. Let stand for 5 minutes before slicing.
MAKES 8 SERVINGS

NOTE: You can ask your butcher to grind a boneless sirloin steak, trimmed of fat, for you.

Nutritional Analysis per Serving:
Calories, 171; Fiber, 1.2 gm; Cholesterol, 57 mg; Sodium, 300 mg
% Calories from: Protein, 52%; Carbohydrate, 18%; Fat, 30% (5.6 gm)

NOTE: Original recipe contains approximately 219 calories, 82 milligrams cholesterol, and 13 grams of fat per serving.

Grand-Prize Chili

The original recipe for this chili won the grand prize at the State Fair of Texas many years ago. Add extra chili powder, cayenne pepper, or jalapeño if you want a hotter chili.

1 tablespoon canola oil
1 pound beef round, trimmed and cut into ¼-inch cubes
1 onion, finely chopped
2 to 3 garlic cloves, minced
1 teaspoon paprika
3 to 4 teaspoons chili powder
1 teaspoon ground cumin
1 teaspoon dried oregano
1 14.5-ounce can Mexican-style stewed tomatoes
1 cup beer or water
1 jalapeño chili, halved and seeded (optional)
1 15-ounce can pinto beans
Finely minced onion for serving (optional)
Grated reduced-fat Cheddar cheese for serving (optional)

In a large saucepan, deep skillet, or Dutch oven, heat the oil over medium-high heat. (Add nonstick cooking spray for good measure.) Add the beef and cook, stirring occasionally, until browned. Add the onion and garlic and sauté for about 3 minutes. Add the paprika, chili powder, cumin, and oregano and stir for 2 minutes. Add the stewed tomatoes, including their liquid, the beer, the jalapeño, and if using, the beans. Stir to combine. Bring to a boil, reduce the heat to low, cover, and simmer for at least 1 hour and up to 2 hours, stirring occasionally.

Sprinkle each serving with minced onion and grated cheese if desired. (This chili can be made up to 3 days in advance; it also freezes well.)

MAKES 5 SERVINGS

Nutritional Analysis per Serving:
Calories, 270; Fiber, 10 gm; Cholesterol, 47 mg; Sodium, 255 mg
% Calories from: Protein, 39%; Carbohydrate, 38%; Fat, 24%
(7 gm)

NOTE: Original recipe contains 629 calories, 132 milligrams
cholesterol, and 43 grams of fat per serving.

Chicken Parmigiana

6 to 8 tablespoons fat-free egg substitute
¾ cup Italian-style or regular bread crumbs
⅛ teaspoon freshly ground pepper
4 boneless, skinless chicken breasts, pounded well with a
      meat mallet to even thickness (or better yet, ask your
      butcher to do it for you)
Olive oil nonstick cooking spray
2 teaspoons canola oil
⅓ cup beer, sherry, or white wine (optional)
1½ cups marinara sauce, homemade (recipe follows) or
      bottled
1 cup grated low-fat mozzarella cheese (or 4 ounces,
      thinly sliced)
3 tablespoons grated Parmesan cheese

Put the egg substitute in a pie plate. On waxed paper, blend the bread crumbs with the pepper. Dip the chicken breasts first in the egg substitute, then in the bread crumbs, then repeat to coat well. Set each piece of chicken aside on a plate.

Coat a large heavy nonstick skillet generously with olive oil nonstick cooking spray. Add the oil and heat over medium-high heat until hot. Add the chicken and brown on the bottom, about 5 minutes. Spray the tops of the chicken with nonstick cooking spray, flip over, and brown on the second side, about 5 minutes. Add the beer if the pan seems dry.

When the chicken is browned on both sides, spoon the sauce over each breast, top with the mozzarella, and sprinkle with the Parmesan. Reduce the heat to low, cover, and continue cooking for about 5 minutes, or until the cheese is melted.

MAKES 4 SERVINGS

Nutritional Analysis per Serving:
Calories, 370; Fiber, 3 gm; Cholesterol, 89 mg; Sodium, 655 mg
% Calories from: Protein, 45%; Carbohydrate, 27%; Fat, 28%
(11.5 gm)

NOTE: Original recipe (using veal) contains 669 calories, 250 milligrams cholesterol, and 41 grams of fat per serving.

Marinara Sauce

*1½ cups canned crushed tomatoes (or 1¼ cups canned
        tomatoes plus ¼ cup tomato paste)*
2 garlic cloves, minced
½ onion, chopped
2 teaspoons sugar
1½ teaspoons dried basil or oregano
Salt to taste (optional)

Combine all the ingredients except the salt in a medium saucepan and simmer for about 20 minutes. Add salt to taste if desired.

Chicago-Style Pizza

When I made this for my daughters for the first time, instead of calling it just "pizza" I told them it was "pizza pie." I didn't want them to expect the thin-crusted, tomato-sauce-topped-with-cheese type of pizza. This style of pizza is completely different. Maybe the biggest difference is that with Chicago-Style Pizza, one slice is usually enough!

2 cups canned crushed tomatoes in puree (I like S&W's crushed tomatoes in a thick, rich puree), 1 28-ounce can Italian plum tomatoes, drained and crushed with a fork, or 2 14.5-ounce cans Italian-style stewed tomatoes, drained
4 garlic cloves, minced
2 tablespoons minced fresh basil or oregano or 2 teaspoons dried
Basic Pizza Dough (recipe follows)
Olive oil nonstick cooking spray
3 cups grated low-fat mozzarella (about 12 ounces)
1/2 cup grated Parmesan cheese
8 to 12 ounces light sausage (I like Jimmy Dean light sausage, cooked and crumbled) (optional) (see first Note)

Preheat the oven to 475 degrees. Combine the tomatoes, garlic, and herbs. Cover and set aside.

Press the dough over the bottom and partway up the sides of a 15-inch deep-dish pizza pan (or divide in half and press into two 9-inch cake pans). Cover with plastic wrap and let rise in a warm place for about 20 minutes.

Prick the bottom of the dough all over with a fork and bake for about 4 minutes. Spray the crust generously with olive oil nonstick cooking spray. Spread the mozzarella cheese over the crust, then spoon the tomatoes on top. Sprinkle with the Parmesan cheese and then with the sausage if using.

Bake on the bottom oven rack for 5 minutes, then move to a rack in the upper third of the oven and bake until the crust is lightly browned and the cheese is bubbly, about 30 minutes longer. MAKES 6 SERVINGS

NOTE: You can use other items to top the tomatoes instead of sausage, such as fresh spinach, sautéed mushrooms or onions, etc.

Nutritional Analysis per Serving:
Calories, 700; Fiber, 5 gm; Cholesterol, 21 mg; Sodium, 1190 mg
% Calories from: Protein, 20%; Carbohydrate, 60%; Fat, 20%
(15.5 gm)

NOTE: Original recipe contains approximately 1075 calories, 86 milligrams cholesterol, and 56 grams of fat per serving.

Basic Pizza Dough

1³⁄₄ cups warm water
1 tablespoon sugar
1 package (1 tablespoon) active dry yeast
About 6 cups unbleached all-purpose flour
3 tablespoons olive oil
1¹⁄₂ teaspoons salt

Pour the water into a large bowl. Add the sugar and yeast, stir until dissolved, and let sit until foamy, about 5 minutes. When the yeast is active, stir in 1 cup of the flour. Stir in the olive oil and salt. Add another 4¹⁄₂ cups flour and mix until the dough forms a ball. Sprinkle about ¹⁄₂ cup flour onto a work surface and knead the dough until smooth and elastic, adding more flour only to keep it from being too sticky.

Green Chili

This recipe was suggested by the *Denver Post* Food Editor, but a recipe for green chili is easy to find in many Southwestern cookbooks. To make this low in fat, I cut down on the oil called for and used the pork cut lowest in fat—the tenderloin. The meat comes out nice and tender and the roasted peppers swimming in the tomato-based chili add a beautiful color and a wonderful flavor. This recipe is now a regular in my kitchen! I like things "warm," not "hot," in terms of spices. If you like it hot, add a little more pepper, a few more chiles, and a dash of Tabasco.

6 to 8 Anaheim chiles, quartered and seeded
1 tablespoon canola oil
1½ pounds pork tenderloin, cut into small cubes
1 large onion, coarsely chopped
2 large garlic cloves, minced
½ teaspoon salt, or to taste
½ teaspoon freshly ground pepper, or to taste
1 16-ounce can whole peeled tomatoes, drained and
*   chopped, juice reserved*
1 12-ounce bottle beer
2 tablespoons all-purpose flour
⅓ cup water
Flour tortillas for serving (optional)

Preheat the oven to 450 degrees. Place the chile peppers on a cookie sheet. Roast for about 30 minutes, or until charred. Let cool slightly, then chop.

Meanwhile, heat the oil in a large nonstick skillet or large saucepan over medium heat. Add the pork, onion, garlic, salt, and pepper and sauté until the pork browns, stirring occasionally. Add the tomatoes and the reserved juice, the beer, and the chopped chiles. Stir well, cover the pan, lower the heat, and simmer for 45 minutes.

Blend the flour with the water and stir until smooth. Add to the chili and stir until well blended. Cover and simmer for an additional 15 minutes. Serve with tortillas if desired.

MAKES 4 LARGE SERVINGS

Nutritional Analysis per Serving:

Calories, 350; Fiber, 4 gm; Cholesterol, 100 mg; Sodium, 461 mg % Calories from: Protein, 50%; Carbohydrate, 24%; Fat, 26% (10 gm)

NOTE: Original recipe contains approximately 630 calories, 179 milligrams cholesterol, and 35 grams of fat per serving.

Three-Step Cheese Steak Sandwich

All right, I admit I had never tasted one of these before I started working on this book. Being born and raised in California, I had heard cheese steak mentioned once or twice—but as far as I knew, it was a steak sandwich made with Philadelphia cream cheese! Since I live on the other side of the country, I had no choice but to trust that the Philadelphia Cheese Steak Sandwich shop near my house was authentic (yes, California actually has a few of these restaurants). Based on my one-time sandwich experience, I whipped up a quick cheese steak sandwich look-alike recipe. Hope you like it.

1 large onion, thinly sliced
1 green bell pepper, thinly sliced (optional)
1/3 cup beer, beef broth, chicken broth, or water (optional)
1 1/2 teaspoons olive oil
1 pound beef round or top round, sliced paper-thin (ask
    your butcher to slice it for you)
Freshly ground pepper
1/2 teaspoon Tabasco, or more to taste
1/2 to 1 teaspoon Worcestershire sauce
2 to 2 1/2 tablespoons Pickapeppa sauce (found in large
    supermarkets with the steak sauce)
2 ounces part-skim mozzarella or reduced-fat Monterey
    Jack, or provolone, thinly sliced
4 sandwich rolls (hoagie, po-boy, submarine, or even giant
    hot dog buns will do)

Heat a medium or large heavy nonstick skillet over medium heat. Spray generously with nonstick cooking spray. Sauté the onion rings, and the bell pepper if desired, adding beer, if desired, as needed for moisture. Continue cooking, stirring occasionally, until the onions caramelize. Remove from the pan and set aside.

Add the olive oil to the pan and heat over medium-high heat until hot. Season the beef with pepper, add to the pan and cook, stirring, until the meat browns. Add the onions and the Tabasco, Worcestershire, and Pickapeppa sauces, stir, and cook until heated through. Turn off the heat.

In the pan, divide the beef/onion mixture into 3 portions. Top each with sliced cheese. Cover the pan and let sit to melt the cheese. Transfer to the rolls and serve.

MAKES 4 SANDWICHES

Nutritional Analysis per Sandwich:

Calories, 623; Fiber, 3.5 gm; Cholesterol, 66 mg; Sodium, 812 mg
% Calories from: Protein, 26%; Carbohydrate, 50%; Fat, 24% (17 gm)

NOTE: Original recipe contains 868 calories, 131 milligrams cholesterol, and 40 grams of fat per sandwich.

Chicken-Fried Steak with Cream Gravy

Chicken-fried steak is another food I had never eaten until I began writing this book. But after a long conversation with a Southern butcher, I felt prepared to tackle my first low-fat chicken-fried steak. And the first try was the charm—even my two-year-old ate it right up, gravy and all. You can dredge the steaks in flour, then dip in egg, and then dredge in flour again, or you can dredge in bread crumbs instead of flour the second time. I'm partial to the bread crumbs.

1 egg
¼ cup fat-free egg substitute
¾ cup evaporated skimmed milk
1½ tablespoons all-purpose flour plus flour for dredging
Bread crumbs for dredging (optional)
1 tablespoon canola oil
4 cube steaks, trimmed of visible fat, or 1 round steak (about
    1⅓ pounds), trimmed of visible fat and tenderized by
    your butcher
Salt (optional) and freshly ground pepper to taste
Canola nonstick cooking spray
3 tablespoons half-and-half
¾ cup water

In a small bowl, beat the egg with the egg substitute and ¼ cup of the evaporated skim milk. Spread flour for dredging in another bowl and place the bread crumbs in a separate bowl if using.

Heat the oil in a large heavy nonstick skillet, tilting the pan to coat the bottom, until very hot. Sprinkle the steaks with salt, if using, and pepper. Dip both sides of the steak first in the flour, then in the egg mixture, then in the flour or bread crumbs, coating well.

When the oil is very hot, add the steaks to the pan and fry for 4 minutes, or until golden brown on the bottom. Spray the tops of the steaks with nonstick cooking spray, flip the steaks over with a spatula, and fry on the other side for about 4 to 5 minutes, until golden on bottom. Place the steaks in a baking pan and keep warm in a 200-degree oven.

To make the gravy, add the half-and-half cream to the skillet, loosening the browned bits from the bottom of the pan with the spatula. Slowly add the remaining 1/2 cup evaporated skim milk. In a small bowl, blend the 1 1/2 tablespoons flour with 1/4 cup of the water. Slowly add the remaining 1/2 cup water, stirring until blended and smooth. Add to the skillet and cook over low heat, stirring constantly, until thickened to the desired consistency, a few minutes. Add salt if using and pepper to taste. Serve the chicken-fried steaks with rice or mashed potatoes and the gravy.
MAKES 4 SERVINGS

Nutritional Analysis per Serving (with mashed potatoes):
Calories, 329; Fiber, 0.5 gm; Cholesterol, 109 mg; Sodium, 178 mg
% Calories from: Protein, 49%; Carbohydrate, 18%; Fat, 33% (11.8 gm)
(When each serving is served with 1/2 cup of cooked rice instead of potatoes, the % calories from fat is reduced to 24% and the calories are increased to 461.)

NOTE: Original recipe contains 749 calories, 329 milligrams cholesterol, and 53 grams of fat per serving.

Country Pot Roast

Slow cooking makes this roast tender, and there's lots of creamy (low-fat) gravy.

1 3- to 5-pound center-cut cross-rib (shoulder) roast,
   trimmed of visible fat
1/4 cup all-purpose flour
1 1/2 teaspoons canola oil
1 cup tomato juice or bottled tomato sauce
3 garlic cloves, minced
4 carrots, sliced
2 medium onions, coarsely chopped
1 cup sliced celery
1 teaspoon salt
1 1/2 teaspoons dried oregano
1/4 teaspoon freshly ground pepper

Place the roast on a cutting board or waxed paper and coat with the flour. Heat the oil in a Dutch oven or a large saucepan over medium-high heat. Add the roast and cook until browned on all sides. Add all the remaining ingredients and bring to a boil. Reduce the heat to low, cover the pot, and simmer for 2 to 4 hours, depending on the size of the roast, or until the meat is fork-tender, turning several times.

Transfer the meat to a cutting board. In batches, puree the cooking liquid and vegetables in a blender at high speed. Pour back into the pan or into a serving bowl. Slice the roast and serve with the vegetable gravy.

MAKES AT LEAST 6 SERVINGS

Nutritional Analysis per Serving (based on a 3-pound roast):
Calories, 412; Fiber, 3 gm; Cholesterol, 163 mg; Sodium, 625 mg
% Calories from: Protein, 55%; Carbohydrate, 16%; Fat, 29%
(13 gm)

NOTE: Original recipe contains 606 calories, 163 milligrams cholesterol, and 38 grams of fat per serving.

Cheeseburger Pie

This easy one-dish meal, a lighter version of Bisquick's "Impossible Cheeseburger Pie," makes its own crust.

1 pound ground sirloin (or the leanest ground beef
    you can find)
1½ cups chopped white onions
½ teaspoon salt
¼ teaspoon freshly ground pepper
1 teaspoon dried oregano, crumbled
1½ cups 1% milk
¾ cup Bisquick reduced-fat baking mix
1 egg
½ cup fat-free egg substitute
2 ripe tomatoes, sliced
4 ounces reduced-fat sharp Cheddar cheese, grated

Preheat the oven to 400 degrees. Spray a 9-inch deep-dish pie plate with nonstick cooking spray. In a nonstick frying pan, brown the beef and onions over medium heat, stirring frequently. Stir in the salt and pepper. Spread the mixture in the prepared pie plate. Sprinkle the oregano evenly over the top.

In a large bowl, beat the milk, Bisquick, egg, and egg substitute with an electric mixer on high speed until smooth, 1 to 2 minutes. Pour over the beef mixture. Bake for 25 minutes.

Top the pie with the tomato slices and sprinkle the cheese evenly over the top. Bake until a knife inserted in the center comes out clean, 5 to 8 minutes.

MAKES 6 SERVINGS

Nutritional Analysis per Serving:

Calories, 292; Fiber, 2 gm; Cholesterol, 98 mg; Sodium, 574 mg
% Calories from: Protein, 40%; Carbohydrate, 30%; Fat 30%
(10 gm)

NOTE: Original recipe contains 399 calories, 183 milligrams cholesterol, and 25 grams of fat per serving.

Low-Fat Chicken Marbella

This luscious chicken dish graced thousands of dinner parties after it appeared in *The Silver Palate Cookbook*. This lighter version significantly lowers the cholesterol and fat without losing any of the flavor.

4 boneless, skinless chicken breasts
6 boneless, skinless chicken thighs
1/2 head of garlic, cloves separated, peeled, and pressed,
    or 2 teaspoons garlic powder
1/4 teaspoon freshly ground pepper, to taste
1/4 cup red wine vinegar
2 tablespoons olive oil
1/2 cup pitted prunes
1/4 cup pitted Spanish green olives
1/4 cup capers, including some juice
3 bay leaves
1/2 cup brown sugar
2/3 cup white wine or champagne
2 tablespoons fresh flat-leaf parsley or coriander leaves
6 cups steamed rice

In a large bowl, combine the first 10 ingredients. Cover and let marinate in the refrigerator for at least 2 hours or overnight if possible.

Preheat the oven to 350 degrees. Arrange the chicken in a single layer in a 13 by 9-inch baking pan. Pour the marinade over the chicken. Sprinkle the chicken with the brown sugar and pour the wine evenly over it.

Bake for 30 to 40 minutes, basting frequently with the pan juices, or until the chicken is cooked through. Toss in the parsley. Make a bed of rice on each serving plate. Using a slotted spoon, place the chicken, prunes, olives, and capers on the rice. Spoon the pan juices over the chicken and rice.

Nutritional Analysis per Serving (including rice):
Calories, 548; Fiber, 1 gm; Cholesterol, 74 mg; Sodium, 231 mg
% Calories from: Protein, 23%; Carbohydrate, 58%; Fat, 18%
(10.5 gm)

NOTE: Original recipe contains 538 calories, 124 milligrams cholesterol, and 26.5 grams of fat per serving (*not* including rice).

Cheeseburger Rice

A one-dish supper, perfect for a busy weeknight.

1 pound ground sirloin (or very lean ground beef)
1 onion, chopped
2 cups water
⅔ cup catsup
2 tablespoons prepared mustard
⅛ teaspoon freshly ground pepper
2 cups Minute original instant enriched rice
1 cup (4 ounces) shredded Kraft light natural Cheddar
*   cheese*

In a large nonstick skillet, brown the beef and onion over medium-high heat, stirring frequently. Stir in the water, catsup, mustard, and pepper. Bring to a boil. Stir in the rice, cover, and remove from the heat. Let stand for 5 minutes.

Fluff the rice with a fork. Sprinkle with the cheese, cover, and let stand for 3 minutes, or until the cheese melts.

MAKES 4 SERVINGS

Nutritional Analysis per Serving:
Calories, 494; Fiber, 2.6 gm; Cholesterol, 91 mg; Sodium, 793 mg
% Calories from: Protein, 32%; Carbohydrate, 46%; Fat, 23% (12 gm)

NOTE: Original recipe contains approximately 627 calories and 28 grams of fat per serving.

Chapter 6

Cookies and Bars

Cocoa Crinkle-Top Cookies

I used Nestlé cocoa in place of *all* the chocolate morsels in the original recipe and made some adjustments for moisture and sweetness, and the cookies turned out wonderfully rich and chocolatey!

1½ cups all-purpose flour
1½ teaspoons baking powder
¼ teaspoon salt
¼ cup (½ stick) butter or margarine, softened
2 tablespoons fat-free or light cream cheese, softened
1 cup granulated sugar
2 teaspoons vanilla extract
¼ cup chocolate syrup
⅔ cup Nestlé baking cocoa
1 large egg
¼ cup fat-free egg substitute
½ cup confectioners' sugar

In a small bowl, combine the flour, baking powder, and salt. In a large bowl, cream the butter, cream cheese, granulated sugar, and vanilla. Beat in the chocolate syrup and cocoa. Add the egg and egg substitute, beating well after each addition. Gradually beat in the dry ingredients. Cover; chill until firm, about 1 hour.

Preheat the oven to 350 degrees. Coat two cookie sheets with nonstick cooking spray. Place the confectioners' sugar in a small bowl. Drop the dough by heaping tablespoonfuls into the confectioners' sugar and roll to coat completely with sugar. Place the cookies on the prepared baking sheets 2 inches apart.

Bake, one cookie sheet at a time, in the upper third of the oven for about 12 minutes, or until the edges are set but the centers are still slightly soft. Remove to wire racks to cool completely.

MAKES 20 TO 22 LARGE COOKIES

Nutritional Analysis per Cookie (based on 20 cookies):
Calories, 113; Fiber, 1 gm; Cholesterol, 15 mg; Sodium, 98 mg
% Calories from: Protein, 7%; Carbohydrate, 71%; Fat, 22% (2.9 gm)

NOTE: Original recipe contains 195 calories, 28 milligrams cholesterol, and 9.3 grams of fat (40% calories from fat) per cookie (20 cookies per batch).

Snickerdoodles

This simple cookie has an irresistible sugar and cinnamon flavor and is easy enough to make with your kids.

2¾ cups Gold Medal all-purpose flour
2 teaspoons cream of tartar
1 teaspoon baking soda
¼ teaspoon salt
1½ cups plus 2 tablespoons sugar
½ cup (1 stick) butter or margarine, softened
½ cup fat-free cream cheese
1 large egg
¼ cup fat-free egg substitute
2 teaspoons ground cinnamon

Preheat the oven to 400 degrees. Coat two cookie sheets with nonstick cooking spray. Combine the flour, cream of tartar, baking soda, and salt. In a large bowl, beat together 1½ cups of the sugar, butter, cream cheese, egg, and egg substitute until smooth. Stir in the dry ingredients.

In a small bowl, mix the remaining 2 tablespoons sugar and the cinnamon. Shape the dough by tablespoonfuls into balls (or use a cookie scoop). Roll the balls in the cinnamon mixture and place about 2 inches apart on the prepared cookie sheet.

Bake, one cookie sheet at a time, in the upper third of the oven for about 8 minutes for chewy cookies or 12 minutes for crisp cookies. Immediately transfer from the cookie sheet to a wire rack to cool.

MAKES ABOUT 3 DOZEN LARGE COOKIES

Nutritional Analysis per Cookie:

Calories, 98; Fiber, 0.3 gm; Cholesterol, 13 mg; Sodium, 85 mg
% Calories from: Protein, 7%; Carbohydrate, 68%; Fat, 25% (2.8 gm)

NOTE: Original recipe contains 122 calories, 19 milligrams cholesterol, and 6 grams fat per cookie.

Crisp Cookie Cutouts

This lighter version of a well-loved sugar cookie recipe has a crisp texture and buttery flavor. It's the ideal cookie for decorating at Christmas and Easter.

1 cup C&H granulated sugar
½ cup (1 stick) butter, softened
½ cup fat-free cream cheese
1 large egg
¼ cup fat-free egg substitute
1½ teaspoons vanilla extract
1 teaspoon almond extract
3½ cups all-purpose flour
1 teaspoon salt
½ teaspoon baking powder
½ recipe Vanilla Buttercream Frosting (page 175) (optional)

In a large bowl, beat the sugar, butter, and cream cheese until fluffy. Beat in the egg and egg substitute, vanilla, and almond extract. Combine the flour, salt, and baking powder; stir into the sugar mixture. Cover and chill for 30 minutes.

Preheat the oven to 375 degrees. Coat two cookie sheets with nonstick cooking spray. On a lightly floured board, roll the dough out to an ⅛-inch thickness. Cut out shapes with cookie cutters and place 2 inches apart on the prepared cookie sheets.

Bake, one cookie sheet at a time, in the upper third of the oven for 7 to 9 minutes, or until the edges are lightly browned. Let cool on wire racks. Frost with Vanilla Buttercream Frosting if desired.

MAKES 2½ DOZEN MEDIUM-TO-LARGE COOKIES

Nutritional Analysis per Cookie (analysis with frosting in parentheses if different):
Calories, 108 (156); Cholesterol, 8 mg; Sodium, 114 (143) mg
% Calories from: Protein, 7% (5%); Carbohydrate, 66% (67%);
Fat, 27% (28%) (3 [5] gm per cookie)

NOTE: The original recipe contains 138 calories, 31 milligrams cholesterol, and 7 grams of fat per cookie without frosting.

The Ultimate Chocolate Chip Cookie

Cutting the fat in chocolate chip cookies is one of the most challenging recipe makeovers because you can't use some of the tricks or fat replacements that you can use in a recipe whose flavor and texture aren't quite as delicate. Everyone has a definite idea of what a chocolate chip cookie tastes like, and most people don't want other flavors from fat replacements interfering with the pure unadulterated bliss of a chocolate chip cookie. I tried to cut the fat as far as I could and still have a cookie that lived up to its name, "the ultimate chocolate chip cookie."

> 7 tablespoons Butter Flavor Crisco (or regular Crisco)
>   all-vegetable shortening
> 1/3 cup fat-free cream cheese
> 1 1/4 cups packed light brown sugar
> 2 tablespoons low-fat buttermilk
> 1 1/2 teaspoons vanilla extract
> 1 1/2 teaspoons butter flavoring
> 1/4 cup fat-free egg substitute (or 1 egg)
> 1 3/4 cups all-purpose flour
> 1 teaspoon salt
> 3/4 teaspoon baking soda
> 1 cup (6 ounces) Hershey's milk chocolate or semisweet
>   chocolate chips
> 1/2 cup coarsely chopped pecans (optional)

Preheat the oven to 375 degrees. Coat two cookie sheets with nonstick cooking spray. In a large bowl, using an electric mixer, beat the Crisco with the cream cheese. Add the brown sugar, buttermilk, and extracts and beat until blended. Beat in the egg substitute.

Combine the flour, salt, and baking soda. Beat into the

creamed mixture just until blended. Stir in the chocolate chips and the pecans if using. Use a cookie scoop (or drop by rounded tablespoonfuls) to form cookies and place 3 inches apart on the prepared baking sheets.

Bake, one cookie sheet at a time, in the upper third of the oven for about 8 minutes for chewy cookies or about 11 minutes for crisp cookies. Cool for 2 minutes on the baking sheets, then remove the cookies to a sheet of foil to cool completely.

MAKES ABOUT 2½ DOZEN LARGE COOKIES

Nutritional Analysis per Cookie:

Calories, 117; Fiber, 0.4 gm; Cholesterol, 0 mg; Sodium, 100 mg
% Calories from: Protein, 4%; Carbohydrate, 58%; Fat, 38% (5 gm)

NOTE: Original recipe contains 152 calories, 7 milligrams cholesterol, and 8.5 grams of fat per cookie.

Classic Oatmeal-Raisin Cookies

I've made many an oatmeal-raisin cookie—but this recipe takes the cake! If you like your oatmeal cookies soft and chewy with a touch of maple flavor, this is the recipe for you.

6 tablespoons butter or margarine, softened
6 tablespoons fat-free or light cream cheese
1 cup packed brown sugar
½ cup granulated sugar
¼ cup low-fat buttermilk
¼ cup fat-free egg substitute
2 tablespoons maple syrup
2 teaspoons vanilla extract
1 cup all-purpose flour
½ teaspoon baking soda
1½ teaspoons ground cinnamon
¼ teaspoon salt
3 cups quick or old-fashioned Quaker oats
1 cup Sun-Maid raisins
½ cup chopped walnuts (optional)

Preheat the oven to 350 degrees. Coat two cookie sheets with nonstick cooking spray. In a large bowl, beat the butter with the cream cheese. Beat in the sugars, buttermilk, egg substitute, maple syrup, and vanilla and beat until light and fluffy. Combine the flour, baking soda, cinnamon, and salt; beat into the butter mixture, mixing well. Stir in the oats, raisins, and the nuts if desired, mixing well.

Use a cookie scoop (or drop by rounded tablespoonfuls) to form cookies and place 2 inches apart on the prepared cookie sheets. For flatter rather than rounded cookies, press each cookie mound down lightly with a spoon, a spatula, or your fingers.

Bake, one cookie sheet at a time, in the upper third of the oven for about 10 minutes, or until lightly browned. Remove the cookies to wire racks to cool completely. Store in an airtight container.

Makes about 32 large cookies

Nutritional Analysis per Cookie:
Calories, 120; Fiber, 1.2 gm; Cholesterol, 5 mg; Sodium, 36 mg
% Calories from: Protein, 7%; Carbohydrate, 73%; Fat, 20% (2.7 gm)

NOTE: Original recipe contains 166 calories, 7 milligrams cholesterol, and 7.8 grams of fat per cookie.

Oatmeal Chocolate Chip Cookies

The wholesome goodness of oatmeal combines with the melting sweetness of chocolate in this chewy cookie.

½ cup (1 stick) butter, softened
½ cup fat-free cream cheese
1 cup packed brown sugar
½ cup granulated sugar
1 large egg
2 tablespoons fat-free egg substitute
¼ cup maple syrup
1 tablespoon vanilla extract
1¾ cups all-purpose flour
1 teaspoon baking soda
½ teaspoon salt
2½ cups quick or old-fashioned Quaker oats
1¼ cups (7½ ounces) milk chocolate or semisweet chocolate
   chips

Preheat the oven to 375 degrees. Coat two cookie sheets with nonstick cooking spray. In a large bowl, beat the butter and cream cheese together. Add the sugars and beat until creamy. Add the egg, egg substitute, maple syrup, and vanilla; beat well. Combine the flour, baking soda, and salt and beat into the egg mixture, mixing well. Stir in the oats and chocolate chips; mix well.

Use a cookie scoop (or drop by rounded tablespoonfuls) to form cookies and place 2 inches apart on the prepared cookie sheets.

Bake, one cookie sheet at a time, in the upper third of the oven for about 9 minutes for chewy cookies or about 12 minutes for crisp cookies. Cool for 1 minute on the cookie sheets, then remove to wire racks. Cool completely.

MAKES 3 DOZEN LARGE COOKIES

Nutritional Analysis per Cookie:

Calories, 142; Fiber, 1 gm; Cholesterol, 13 mg; Sodium, 105 mg
% Calories from: Protein, 6%; Carbohydrate, 62%; Fat, 32% (5 gm)

NOTE: Original recipe contains 180 calories, 26 milligrams cholesterol, and 9 grams of fat per cookie.

Cherry Crunch Cookies

The Pillsbury Bake-Off favorite that inspired this lower-fat version was named Cherry Winks. Sweet cherries in a rich dough and a crunchy cornflake coating make these a winner in anyone's book.

1 cup sugar
6 tablespoons butter, softened, or butter-flavor shortening such as Crisco
6 tablespoons fat-free cream cheese
2 teaspoons vanilla extract
1 large egg
3 tablespoons fat-free egg substitute
2¼ cups all-purpose or unbleached all-purpose Pillsbury flour
1 teaspoon baking powder
½ teaspoon baking soda
½ teaspoon salt
½ cup chopped pecans
1 cup chopped dates or raisins
⅓ cup chopped maraschino cherries, well drained (or glacé cherries)
1½ cups coarsely crushed cornflakes
12 maraschino cherries, drained and quartered (or glacé cherries)

Preheat the oven to 375 degrees. Spray two cookie sheets with nonstick cooking spray. In a large bowl, combine the sugar, butter, cream cheese, vanilla, egg, and egg substitute, using an electric mixer; beat on medium speed until well mixed. In a small bowl, combine the flour, baking powder, baking soda, and salt; mix well. Add to the sugar mixture and beat on low speed until well blended. Stir in the pecans, dates, and chopped cherries. (If desired, cover and refrigerate the dough for 30 to 60 minutes for easier handling.)

Place the crushed cornflakes in a shallow bowl. Using a cookie scoop to measure the dough, or using 1 heaping tablespoon per cookie, shape into balls and coat thoroughly with the cereal. Place 2 inches apart on the prepared cookie sheets. Gently press a cherry piece into the top of each ball.

Bake, one cookie sheet at a time, in the upper third of the oven, for 10 minutes, or until light golden brown. Transfer to wire racks to cool.

MAKES 2 DOZEN LARGE COOKIES

Nutritional Analysis per Cookie:
Calories, 160; Fiber, 1 gm; Cholesterol, 18 mg; Sodium, 161 mg
% Calories from: Protein, 4%; Carbohydrate, 69%; Fat, 27% (4.8 gm)

NOTE: Original recipe contains 190 calories, 33 milligrams cholesterol, and 9.5 grams of fat per cookie.

Peanut Kisses

The original recipe, Peanut Blossoms, was a Pillsbury Bake-Off winner in 1957, and it has been a favorite ever since. The combination of peanut butter and chocolate is a real crowd-pleaser.

1³/₄ cups Pillsbury all-purpose flour
¹/₂ cup granulated sugar
¹/₂ cup packed brown sugar
1 teaspoon baking soda
¹/₂ teaspoon salt
¹/₄ cup (¹/₂ stick) butter, softened, or butter-flavored
*   shortening*
¹/₃ cup creamy peanut butter
¹/₃ cup fat-free cream cheese
2 tablespoons milk
2 teaspoons vanilla extract
1 large egg
Sugar for rolling
About 30 chocolate candy kisses

Preheat the oven to 375 degrees. In a large bowl, using an electric mixer, beat the flour, sugars, baking soda, salt, butter, peanut butter, cream cheese, milk, vanilla, and egg on low speed until a stiff dough forms.

Place the sugar in a small bowl. Using a cookie scoop to measure the dough, turn into balls (or shape into 1¹/₂-inch balls) and roll each ball in the sugar. Place 2 inches apart on ungreased cookie sheets.

Bake, one cookie sheet at a time, in the upper third of the oven for about 10 minutes, or until lightly golden brown (do not overbake). Immediately top each cookie with a kiss, pressing down firmly so the cookies crack around the edges; remove from the cookie sheets and let cool on wire racks.

MAKES ABOUT 2¹/₂ DOZEN LARGE COOKIES

Nutritional Analysis per Cookie:

Calories, 111; Fiber, 1 gm; Cholesterol, 12 mg; Sodium, 86 mg
% Calories from: Protein, 7%; Carbohydrate, 56%; Fat, 37% (4.5 gm)

NOTE: Original recipe contains 152 calories and 8.2 grams of fat per cookie.

Chocolate–Chocolate Chip Oatmeal Cookies

Whoever added cocoa to chocolate chip oatmeal cookies knew what she or he was doing. I've made the original recipe even better by taking out half the fat!

1 1/4 cups all-purpose flour
1/2 cup Nestlé baking cocoa
1 teaspoon baking soda
1/2 teaspoon salt
1/2 cup (1 stick) butter or margarine, softened
1/2 cup fat-free cream cheese
1 cup packed brown sugar
1/2 cup granulated sugar
2 teaspoons vanilla extract
1 large egg
1/4 cup fat-free egg substitute
1 cup (6 ounces) Nestlé Toll House milk chocolate morsels
1 3/4 cup Quaker quick or old-fashioned oats
1/2 cup chopped walnuts (optional)

Preheat the oven to 375 degrees. Coat two cookie sheets with nonstick cooking spray. In a small bowl, combine the flour, cocoa, baking soda, and salt. In a large bowl, cream the butter and cream cheese. Add the sugars and vanilla and blend until smooth. Add the egg and egg substitute, beating well after each addition. Gradually beat in the dry ingredients. Stir in the chocolate morsels, oats, and the walnuts if desired.

Drop by rounded tablespoonfuls, 2 inches apart, onto the prepared cookie sheets. Bake, one cookie sheet at a time, in the upper third of the oven for about 8 to 10 minutes, or until still a little soft in the center for a chewy cookie. Let stand for 2 minutes, then remove to wire racks to cool completely.

MAKES 4¹/₂ DOZEN COOKIES

Nutrition Analysis per Cookie:
Calories, 78; Cholesterol, 8.5 mg; Sodium, 63 mg
% Calories from: Protein, 6%; Carbohydrate, 58%; Fat, 36% (3 gm)

NOTE: Original recipe contains 110 calories, 17 milligrams cholesterol, and 6 grams of fat (48% calories from fat) per cookie.

Best Brownies Made Better

These chewy delights use cocoa powder for deep chocolate flavor and light sour cream and corn syrup for richness without a lot of fat.

1 cup all-purpose flour
1/2 teaspoon baking powder
1/4 teaspoon salt
1/3 cup butter or margarine
7 tablespoons light sour cream
1/4 cup light corn syrup
1 3/4 cups sugar
1 tablespoon vanilla extract
1 large egg
1/2 cup fat-free egg substitute
3/4 cup Hershey's cocoa or Hershey's European-style cocoa
1/3 cup chopped nuts (optional)

Preheat the oven to 350 degrees. Coat a 9-inch square baking pan with nonstick cooking spray.

Combine the flour, baking powder, and salt.

Place the butter in a large microwave-safe bowl. Microwave on the Defrost setting in 30-second intervals until melted. Beat in the sour cream, corn syrup, sugar, and vanilla. Add the egg and egg substitute, beating well after each addition. Add the cocoa, beating until well blended. Add the combined dry ingredients and beat well. Stir in the nuts if desired. Pour the batter into the prepared pan.

Bake in the center of the oven for 25 to 30 minutes, or until the brownies begin to pull away from the sides of the pan. Cool completely in the pan on a wire rack. Cut into bars.

MAKES 25 EXTRA-THICK BROWNIES

Nutritional Analysis per Brownie:
Calories, 118; Fiber, 0.9 gm; Cholesterol, 15.5 mg; Sodium, 87 mg
% Calories from: Protein, 6%; Carbohydrate, 70%; Fat, 24% (3 gm)

NOTE: Original recipe contains 164 calories, 54 milligrams cholesterol, and 9 grams of fat per brownie.

Magic Cookie Bars

I don't think you'll be able to tell the difference between the original and lighter versions of this ever-popular cookie.

1/4 cup diet margarine (I like I Can't Believe It's Not Butter light)
1 1/2 cups graham cracker crumbs (about 8 whole crackers, processed to crumbs)
1 14-ounce can Eagle brand low-fat sweetened condensed milk (not evaporated milk)
1 cup (6 ounces) semisweet chocolate chips
1 cup flaked sweetened coconut
1 cup miniature marshmallows
1/2 cup chopped pecans or walnuts

Preheat the oven to 350 degrees (325 degrees for glass dish). Coat a 9-inch square baking pan with nonstick cooking spray. Add the margarine and place the pan in the oven until the margarine melts. Sprinkle the cracker crumbs over the margarine; pour the sweetened condensed milk evenly over the crumbs. Top with the chocolate chips, coconut, marshmallows, and nuts; press down firmly (THIS IS IMPORTANT!). Bake for 25 to 30 minutes, or until lightly browned on top. Let cool completely on wire racks while still in the pan. Chill if desired. Cut into bars. (These freeze nicely.)

MAKES 25 BARS

Nutritional Analysis per Bar:
Calories, 144; Fiber, 1 gm; Cholesterol, 2 mg; Sodium, 72 mg
% Calories from: Protein, 28%; Carbohydrate, 32%; Fat, 40%
(6.5 gm)

NOTE: Original recipe contains 183 calories, 15 milligrams cholesterol, and 12 grams of fat per bar.

SEVEN-LAYER MAGIC COOKIE BARS: Add 1 cup cut-up caramels (cut
each caramel into 4 pieces; you will need about 16 caramels). (A
cup of caramels adds 9 grams of fat and 497 calories per recipe,
compared to 1 cup of butterscotch chips, which adds more than
800 calories and more than 60 grams of fat.)

Low-Fat Lemon Squares

I changed the original recipe by using a nine-inch square pan (instead of an eight-inch) and I added a bit more lemon filling while keeping the amount of butter crust the same. The original recipe makes sixty-four cookies; I prefer to make twenty-five larger squares.

1 cup Gold Medal all-purpose flour (see first Note)
1/4 cup confectioners' sugar
5 tablespoons diet margarine, melted
1 1/2 cups granulated sugar
2 eggs
1/4 cup light sour cream
1 tablespoon grated lemon zest (optional)
3 tablespoons lemon juice
3/4 teaspoon baking powder
3/8 teaspoon salt
Confectioners' sugar for sprinkling

Preheat the oven to 350 degrees. Coat a 9-inch square baking pan with nonstick cooking spray. In a small bowl, mix the flour, powdered sugar, and melted margarine. Press evenly over the bottom of the pan.

In a large bowl, beat the sugar, eggs, sour cream, the lemon zest if using, the lemon juice, baking powder, and salt until light and fluffy, about 3 minutes. Pour over the crust.

Bake for 35 to 40 minutes, or until the center is firm to the touch. Let cool on a wire rack while still in the pan. Sprinkle with confectioners' sugar. Cut into squares.

MAKES 25 SQUARES

NOTE: If using self-rising flour, omit the baking powder and salt.

Nutritional Analysis per Square:
Calories, 91; Cholesterol, 17 mg; Sodium, 75 mg
% Calories from: Protein, 5%; Carbohydrate, 73%; Fat, 22% (2.2 gm)

NOTE: Original recipe (with less lemon filling) contains 92 calories and 4 grams of fat (40% calories from fat) per square.

Mom Magee's Chewy Chocolate Cookies

These are a favorite at my house, and I bet they will be at yours too.

5 tablespoons butter, softened
7 tablespoons fat-free cream cheese
2 cups sugar
1 egg
2 egg whites
1 tablespoon vanilla extract
2 cups all-purpose flour
3/4 cup unsweetened cocoa
1 teaspoon baking soda
1/2 teaspoon salt
1 1/3 cups (8 ounces) semisweet chocolate chips
1 cup chopped walnuts (optional)

Preheat the oven to 350 degrees. Coat two cookie sheets with nonstick cooking spray.

In a large bowl, cream the butter and cream cheese together. Add the sugar and beat until creamy. Add the egg, egg whites, and vanilla and beat until smooth. Combine the flour, cocoa, baking soda, and salt in a medium bowl. Add to the butter mixture and beat until blended. Stir in the chocolate chips and the walnuts if desired. Drop by teaspoonfuls onto the prepared cookie sheets.

Bake, one cookie sheet at a time, in the top third of the oven, for about 8 minutes; do not overbake. Remove from cookie sheet and let cool on a wire rack.

MAKES ABOUT 4 DOZEN COOKIES

NOTE: To make larger cookies, use a cookie scoop to form cookies. Bake for about 10 minutes. (This will yield about 2 1/2 dozen cookies.)

Nutritional Analysis per Cookie (48 cookies per recipe):
Calories, 93; Fiber, 0.7 gm; Cholesterol, 7.6 mg; Sodium, 66 mg
% Calories from: Protein, 7%; Carbohydrate, 61%; Fat, 32% (3
gm)

NOTE: Original recipe contains 120 calories, 17 milligrams cholesterol, and 6 grams of fat per cookie.

Chapter 7

Cakes and Cheesecakes

Better-Than-Sex Cake #1

According to the *San Francisco Chronicle*, two desserts have been given the hard-to-live-up-to name "Better-Than-Sex Cake." But one isn't a cake at all—it's more like a pudding pie. I lightened them both up and tested them on two groups of people, expecting that one of them would emerge as the dessert best suited for that promiseful recipe title. But in both test groups, half preferred the cake and half most enjoyed the pudding pie. So I give you both recipes. (But if you ask me, neither quite lives up to the name!) Oh, incidentally, the chocolate cake tastes even better the day *after* you make it.

1 cup (6 ounces) semisweet chocolate chips (optional)
½ cup pecans, toasted and chopped (optional)
1 package chocolate cake mix (2-layer size—517 grams)
1 4-ounce package instant chocolate pudding mix
1 cup light or nonfat sour cream
2 eggs
½ cup fat-free egg substitute
½ cup chocolate syrup
¼ cup Kahlúa, brewed espresso, or water
1½ teaspoons vanilla extract
Dark Chocolate Glaze (recipe follows)

Preheat the oven to 350 degrees. Place an oven rack in the lowest position if using a tube or Bundt pan or the middle position if using a cake pan. Coat a 10-inch tube, 10-inch Bundt, or 13 x 9-inch baking pan with nonstick cooking spray.

If using chocolate chips and nuts, toss them with 1 tablespoon of the cake mix; set aside. Combine the (remaining) cake mix, pudding mix, sour cream, eggs, egg substitute, chocolate syrup, Kahlúa and vanilla in a large bowl and beat for 3 minutes with an electric mixer on medium speed. Fold in the nuts and chocolate chips if using.

Turn the batter into the prepared pan and bake for 50 to 60 minutes, or until a toothpick inserted in the center comes out clean. Transfer to a wire rack to cool; if you used a tube or Bundt pan, let cool for 15 minutes in the pan, then turn the cake out onto a rack to cool completely before glazing.

Once the cake is cool, pour the glaze over the top and let it drip down the sides of the cake, or if using the baking pan just pour over the top.

Makes 16 servings

Chocolate Glaze

1¹/₃ cups (8 ounces) semisweet chocolate chips
2 tablespoons Kahlúa, Bailey's light Irish cream, or other
    liqueur
¹/₃ cup water
1 teaspoon vanilla extract

Combine the chocolate chips, liqueur, and water in the top of a double boiler set over simmering water. Stir until melted and shiny. Take off the heat and stir in the vanilla. Let cool to room temperature, or chill until thickened.

Nutritional Analysis per Serving:

Calories, 480; Fiber, 1.3 gm; Cholesterol, 28 mg; Sodium, 472 mg % Calories from: Protein, 6%; Carbohydrate, 64%; Fat, 30% (16 gm)

NOTE: The original recipe contains 550 calories, 60 milligrams cholesterol, and 37 grams of fat per serving.

Better-Than-Sex Cake #2

1 cup all-purpose flour
½ cup chopped pecans
¼ cup better-tasting diet margarine (I like I Can't Believe
   It's Not Butter light)
1 tablespoon low-fat buttermilk
1 cup fat-free or light cream cheese, softened
1 cup confectioners' sugar
1 8-ounce container (3¼ cups) light Cool Whip
2¼ cups 1% milk
2 tablespoons liqueur of your choice, such as Grand Marnier
   or light Bailey's Irish cream
2 3½-ounce packages instant chocolate pudding mix
Cocoa or grated chocolate for dusting (optional)

Preheat the oven to 350 degrees. Coat a 9-inch square baking pan with nonstick cooking spray. Combine the flour, pecans, diet margarine, and buttermilk in a food processor and pulse briefly to mix. Press evenly over the bottom of the prepared pan. Bake for 15 to 20 minutes, or until lightly brown. Set aside to cool.

Combine the cream cheese and sugar in a large bowl and beat with an electric or hand-held mixer until smooth. Add 2 cups of the Cool Whip and beat on low speed until blended. Cover and refrigerate until needed.

In another large bowl, combine the milk, liqueur, and pudding mix. Beat on low speed for 3 minutes, or until thickened. Fold in the remaining 1¼ cups Cool Whip. Spread the pudding mixture over the cooled crust. Spread the cream cheese mixture evenly over the chocolate layer. Refrigerate until read to serve.

Just before serving, dust the top with sifted cocoa or grated chocolate if desired.

Makes 16 servings

Nutritional Analysis per Serving:
Calories, 181; Fiber, 0.5 gm; Cholesterol, 3 mg; Sodium, 323 mg
% Calories from: Protein, 9%; Carbohydrate, 61%; Fat, 30% (6 gm)

NOTE: Original recipe contains 370 calories, 29 milligrams choles-terol, and 22 grams of fat per serving.

Vanilla Buttercream Frosting

Substituting fat-free cream cheese for half the butter in the traditional buttercream frosting recipe doesn't save calories, but it does cut the fat in half.

¼ cup (½ stick) butter, softened
¼ cup fat-free cream cheese, softened
5 cups C&H confectioners' sugar
Pinch of salt
3 tablespoons milk
1 teaspoon vanilla extract

In a large bowl, beat in the butter and cream cheese with an electric mixer until blended and smooth, scraping the sides often. Add the remaining ingredients and beat until smooth and creamy. MAKES AT LEAST 12 SERVINGS

Nutritional Analysis per Serving (12 servings per recipe):
Calories, 200; Cholesterol, 10 mg; Sodium, 71 mg
% Calories from: Protein, 2%; Carbohydrate, 80%; Fat, 18% (4 gm)

NOTE: Original recipe contains 200 calories, 21 milligrams cholesterol, and 8 grams of fat per serving.

Chocolate Lover's Frosting

The combination of cocoa and chocolate syrup gives this frosting real depth of chocolate flavor.

3 cups sifted confectioners' sugar
⅔ cup Nestlé Toll House baking cocoa
⅓ cup diet margarine (I like I Can't Believe It's Not Butter light)
3 tablespoons light cream cheese
2 tablespoons chocolate syrup
2 tablespoons 1% milk
1 teaspoon vanilla extract

In a medium bowl, beat 1 cup of the confectioners' sugar, the cocoa, diet margarine, cream cheese, chocolate syrup, milk, and vanilla until creamy. Gradually beat in the remaining 2 cups sugar until smooth.

MAKES ABOUT 2 CUPS

Nutritional Analysis per Serving (10 servings per recipe):
Calories, 175; Fiber, 2; Cholesterol, about 2.5 mg (varies by brand of margarine); Sodium, 55 mg
% Calories from: Protein, 4%; Carbohydrate, 75%; Fat, 21% (4.5 gm)

NOTE: Original recipe contains 217 calories and 10.6 grams fat per serving.

Rum Cake

This is so dense, moist, and deeply satisfying, you won't believe you're eating a lightened-up dessert. Use dark rum for the best flavor.

1/2 cup chopped pecans or walnuts
1 box yellow cake mix (not the type with pudding in the
    mix) (2-layer size—517 grams)
1 3.4-ounce package instant vanilla pudding and pie filling
    (4-serving size)
2 large eggs
1/3 cup fat-free egg substitute
1/3 cup pineapple juice
1/2 cup light sour cream
1/2 cup plus 3 tablespoons Bacardi dark rum

GLAZE
2 tablespoons butter
1/2 cup plus 2 tablespoons Bacardi dark rum
2/3 cup sugar

Preheat the oven to 325 degrees. Coat a 10-inch tube pan or 12-cup Bundt pan with nonstick cooking spray. Sprinkle the nuts over the bottom of the pan. In a large bowl, combine all the remaining cake ingredients and beat until blended. Pour the batter over the nuts.

Bake in the center of the oven for 50 to 60 minutes or until a cake tester inserted in the center comes out clean. Let the cake cool completely, then invert it onto a serving plate.

To make the glaze, melt the butter in a small saucepan. Stir in 1/2 cup of the rum and the sugar. Boil for 4 minutes, stirring constantly. Remove from the heat and stir in the remaining 2 tablespoons rum. Let cool slightly before using.

Prick the top of the cake all over with a skewer. Spoon or brush some of the glaze evenly over the top and sides of the cake. Allow the cake to absorb the glaze, then repeat until all the glaze is used.

Makes 12 servings

Nutritional Analysis per Serving:
Calories, 369; Fiber, 0.5 gm; Cholesterol, 42 mg; Sodium, 433 mg
% Calories from: Protein, 7%; Carbohydrate, 68%; Fat, 25% (10 gm)

NOTE: Original recipe contains 550 calories, 91 milligrams cholesterol, and 28.5 grams of fat per serving.

Pound Cake

Whether you enjoy this cake plain, as a base for strawberry short-cake, or toasted for midafternoon tea, you won't be disappointed in the taste—or in the number of calories and fat grams you save.

> *4 cups C&H confectioners' sugar*
> *½ cup (1 stick) butter or margarine, softened*
> *½ cup fat-free cream cheese, softened*
> *½ cup light sour cream*
> *1 tablespoon vanilla extract*
> *3 large eggs*
> *½ cup fat-free egg substitute*
> *3 cups cake flour or 2⅔ cups all-purpose flour*
> *¼ teaspoon salt*

Preheat the oven to 350 degrees. Coat a 10-inch tube pan with nonstick cooking spray. In a large bowl, beat the sugar, butter, cream cheese, sour cream, and vanilla until fluffy. Beat in the eggs one at a time. Beat in the egg substitute ¼ cup at a time. Combine the flour and salt; beat into the sugar mixture. Pour the batter into the prepared pan.

Bake for 1 hour or until a toothpick inserted in the center of the cake comes out clean. Let cool slightly before unmolding, then turn out onto a wire rack to cool.

MAKE 16 SERVINGS

Nutritional Analysis per Serving:
Calories, 243; Fiber, 0.5 gm; Cholesterol, 57 mg; Sodium ,160 mg
% Calories from: Protein, 9%; Carbohydrate, 65%; Fat, 26% (7 gm)

NOTE: Original recipe contains 351 calories, 126 milligrams cho-lesterol, and 19 grams of fat per serving.

Tunnel-of-Fudge Cake

Apparently the tunnel of fudge is a tunnel of fat, because when I reduced the fat in the cake batter, the tunnel of fudge disappeared. So I went to "Plan B"—simulating a tunnel of fudge.

FUDGE TUNNEL
¾ cup fat-free or light cream cheese
¼ cup chocolate syrup
3 tablespoons unsweetened cocoa
2 tablespoons sugar

CAKE
1½ cups granulated sugar
½ cup (1 stick) butter, softened
⅓ cup fat-free cream cheese, softened
⅓ cup chocolate syrup
3 large eggs
½ cup fat-free egg substitute
1½ cups confectioners' sugar
2¼ cups all-purpose or unbleached all-purpose flour
¾ cup unsweetened cocoa
1 cup chopped walnuts (optional)

GLAZE
¾ cup confectioners' sugar
¼ cup unsweetened cocoa
1½ to 2 tablespoons milk or Kahlúa

Preheat the oven to 350 degrees. Coat a 9-inch tube or 10-inch Bundt pan with nonstick cooking spray. Combine all the fudge tunnel ingredients in a small bowl and blend with an electric mixer, or process in a food processor until blended. Set aside.

To make the cake batter, in a large bowl, beat the sugar,

butter, and cheese until light and fluffy. Beat in the chocolate syrup. Add the eggs one at a time, beating well after each addition. Add the egg substitute ¼ cup at a time, beating well after each addition. Gradually add the confectioners' sugar and beat until blended. Stir in the flour, cocoa, and the walnuts if desired.

Spoon half of the batter into the prepared pan, spreading it evenly. Spoon the fudge tunnel mixture into the center of the batter, making a ring. Top with the remaining cake batter and spread it evenly.

Bake in the center of the oven for about 50 to 55 minutes, until top springs back when lightly touched. Cool in the pan on a wire rack for 1 hour, then invert onto a serving plate. Cool completely.

To make the glaze, in a small bowl, blend the confectioners' sugar and cocoa. Stir in enough milk to reach a drizzling consistency. Spoon the glaze over the cake, allowing some to run down the sides. Let the glaze set, then store the cake tightly covered.

MAKES 16 SERVINGS

Nutritional Analysis per Serving:
Calories, 340; Fiber, 3.6 gm; Cholesterol, 56 mg; Sodium, 239 mg
% Calories from: Protein, 9%; Carbohydrate, 70%; Fat, 21% (8 gm)

NOTE: Original recipe contains 560 calories, 100 milligrams cholesterol, and 33 grams of fat per serving.

Lemon Chiffon Cake

When it was introduced in 1948, it was the cake discovery of the century. Almost fifty years later, it is still one of Betty Crocker's most requested recipes. The original was lighter than many traditional butter-and-egg-laden cakes; my version brings the fat and calorie count down even further.

2 cups all-purpose flour
1¼ cups sugar
1 tablespoon baking powder
1 teaspoon salt
¼ cup canola oil
¼ cup light corn syrup
3 large egg yolks
½ cup fat-free egg substitute
¾ cup cold water
2 teaspoons grated lemon zest
2 teaspoons vanilla extract
7 large egg whites
½ teaspoon cream of tartar
Lemon Butter Frosting (recipe follows)

Preheat the oven to 325 degrees. Mix the flour, sugar, baking powder, and salt in a large bowl. Make a well in the center and add, in this order, the oil, corn syrup, egg yolks, egg substitute, water, lemon zest, and vanilla. Beat with a spoon until smooth.

In a large bowl, beat the egg whites and cream of tartar with an electric mixer on high speed until stiff peaks form. Pour the egg yolk mixture gradually over the beaten egg whites, gently folding it in with a rubber spatula just until blended. Pour the batter into an ungreased 10-inch tube pan.

Bake until the top springs back when lightly touched, about

1 hour and 15 minutes. Invert the pan on a funnel or a bottle with a long neck and let cool completely.

Remove the cake from the pan and place on a serving plate. Frost with the lemon butter frosting.

MAKES 16 SERVINGS

Lemon Butter Frosting

1/3 cup diet margarine (I like I Can't Believe It's Not Butter light), or 2 1/2 tablespoons softened butter blended with 2 1/2 tablespoons fat-free cream cheese
3 cups confectioners' sugar
1/2 teaspoon grated lemon zest
1 1/2 to 2 tablespoons lemon juice

Combine the margarine and sugar in a large bowl. Beat in the lemon zest and lemon juice and beat until of spreading consistency.

Nutritional Analysis per Serving:
Calories, 255; Fiber, 0.5 gm; Cholesterol, 40 mg; Sodium, 275 mg
% Calories from: Protein, 6%; Carbohydrate, 73%; Fat, 21% (6.5 gm)

NOTE: Original recipe contains 330 calories, 103 milligrams cholesterol, and 13 grams of fat (35% calories from fat) per serving.

Crumb Coffee Cake with Broiled Topping

Since it was first introduced in a 1951 ad, Velvet Crumb Cake has been a favorite recipe of Bisquick users. Although General Mills touts this cake as a dessert, it makes a dynamite coffee or brunch cake. By using reduced-fat Bisquick and low-fat dairy products, I've cut the fat grams per serving almost by half.

CAKE

1½ cups Bisquick reduced-fat baking mix
½ cup sugar
1 large egg or ¼ cup fat-free egg substitute
½ cup 1% milk
2 tablespoons light sour cream
1½ teaspoons vanilla extract

TOPPING

½ cup flaked sweetened coconut
1 tablespoon all-purpose flour
⅓ cup packed brown sugar
¼ cup chopped walnuts or pecans
3 tablespoons diet margarine, softened
2 tablespoons 1% milk

Preheat the oven to 350 degrees. Spray an 8-inch square baking pan or a 9-inch round cake pan with nonstick cooking spray. Combine all the coffee cake ingredients in a large bowl and beat with an electric mixer on low speed for about 30 seconds, scraping the sides of the bowl frequently. Beat on medium speed for 3 minutes, scraping the sides of the bowl occasionally. Pour into the prepared pan.

Bake for about 25 to 30 minutes, or until a toothpick inserted in the center comes out clean.

Meanwhile, to make the broiled topping, combine all the ingredients in a small bowl and mix well.

Spread the warm cake with the broiled topping mixture. Set the oven control to Broil, place the cake 3 inches from the heat and broil for about 2 minutes, or until the topping is golden brown. MAKES 8 SERVINGS

Nutritional Analysis per Serving:
Calories, 260; Fiber, 2 gm; Cholesterol, 28 mg; Sodium, 340 mg
% Calories from: Protein, 6%; Carbohydrate, 64%; Fat, 30% (8.5 gm)

NOTE: Original recipe contains 300 calories, 30 milligrams cholesterol, and 15 grams of fat per serving.

Gelatin Poke Cake

My version of this well-known cake is just as pretty to look at as the original but has almost two thirds less fat per serving. How's that for having your cake and eating it too?

> 1 package (2-layer size—517 grams) white cake mix or
> pudding-included white cake mix
> 1/2 cup fat-free egg substitute
> 1/3 cup light or nonfat sour cream
> 1 package (4-serving size) Jell-O sugar-free gelatin (any
> flavor—lemon or lime, cherry, raspberry, or strawberry
> all work great!)
> 1 cup boiling water
> 1/2 cup cold water
> 2 to 3 cups light Cool Whip
> Fresh fruit for garnish (optional)

Preheat the oven to 350 degrees. Coat a 13 x 9-inch baking pan with nonstick cooking spray. In a large bowl, prepare the cake mix, using the egg substitute in place of the 3 eggs called for and the sour cream in place of the oil called for, and adding the amount of water called for on the box. Pour into the prepared pan.

Bake for 30 to 35 minutes, or until a fork or toothpick inserted in the center comes out clean. Cool the cake in the pan for 15 minutes; then pierce the top of the cake with a kitchen fork at 1/2-inch intervals.

Meanwhile, dissolve in a medium bowl the gelatin in the boiling water. Add the cold water.

Carefully pour the gelatin mixture over the cake. Chill for about 3 hours. Spread the Cool Whip over the top and garnish with fresh fruit if desired.

Makes 12 servings

Nutritional Analysis per Serving (using Duncan Hines Moist Deluxe White Cake Mix and based on 2¹/₂ cups light Cool Whip):

Calories, 220; Cholesterol, 0 mg; Sodium, 260 mg

% Calories from: Protein, 7%; Carbohydrate, 71%; Fat, 22% (5.5 gm)

NOTE: Original recipe contains 345 calories, 53 milligrams cholesterol, and 15 grams of fat per serving.

Fresh Orange Cake with
Walnut Cinnamon-Sugar Topping

The original recipe for Orange Kiss-Me Cake is from the 1950 Pillsbury Bake-Off, and Pillsbury still gets requests for it. No one cared how many fat grams a recipe had in the fifties; we're more careful now. My light version of Kiss-Me Cake gets only 20 percent of its calories from fat.

CAKE

1 orange
1 cup raisins
2 cups Pillsbury Best all-purpose or unbleached all-purpose
    flour
1 cup sugar
1 teaspoon baking soda
1 teaspoon salt
1 cup 1% milk
¼ cup (½ stick) margarine or butter, softened, or ¼ cup
    shortening
¼ cup light or nonfat sour cream
1 large egg
¼ cup fat-free egg substitute

TOPPING

⅓ cup fresh orange juice (reserved from cake)
¼ cup sugar
1 teaspoon ground cinnamon
¼ cup finely chopped walnuts

Preheat the oven to 350 degrees. Coat a 13 by 9-inch baking pan with nonstick cooking spray. Squeeze ⅓ cup of juice from the orange and reserve for the topping. In a blender or food processor, grind together the orange peel and pulp and the raisins until chunky. Set aside.

In a large bowl, combine all the remaining cake ingredients and beat with an electric mixer on low speed until evenly moistened. Beat for 3 minutes on medium speed. Stir in the orange-raisin mixture. Pour the batter into the prepared pan.

Bake for about 35 minutes, or until a toothpick inserted in the center comes out clean.

Drizzle the reserved orange juice over the warm cake. In a small bowl, combine the sugar and cinnamon; mix well. Stir in the walnuts; sprinkle over the cake.

MAKES 12 TO 16 SERVINGS

Nutritional Analysis per Serving (16 servings per recipe):
Calories, 210; Fiber, 1.5 gm; Cholesterol, 22 mg; Sodium, 240 mg
% Calories from: Protein, 8%; Carbohydrate, 72%; Fat, 20% (4.5 gm)

NOTE: Original recipe contains 250 calories and 10 grams of fat (36% calories from fat) per serving.

Deep Dark Chocolate Cake

This version of the recipe that appears on Hershey's cocoa tins is just as dark and deeply flavored as the original.

2 cups sugar
1³/₄ cups all-purpose flour
³/₄ cup Hershey's cocoa or Hershey's European-style cocoa
1¹/₂ teaspoon baking powder
1¹/₂ teaspoon baking soda
1 teaspoon salt
1 large egg
¹/₄ cup fat-free egg substitute
1 cup 1% milk
¹/₄ cup vegetable oil
¹/₄ cup light or nonfat sour cream
1 tablespoon pure vanilla extract
1 cup boiling water
One-Bowl Buttercream Frosting (recipe follows)

Preheat the oven to 350 degrees. Coat a 13 by 9-inch baking pan with nonstick cooking spray. In a large bowl, stir together the sugar, flour, cocoa, baking powder, baking soda, and salt. Add the egg and egg substitute, milk, oil, sour cream, and vanilla and beat with an electric mixer on medium speed for 2 minutes. Stir in the boiling water (the batter will be thin). Pour the batter into the prepared pan.

Bake for approximately 35 minutes, or until a wooden pick inserted in the center comes out clean. Cool completely before frosting (with buttercream frosting).
MAKES 12 SERVINGS

One-Bowl Buttercream Frosting

2²/₃ cups powdered sugar
¹/₂ cup Hershey's cocoa
6 tablespoons diet margarine spread
¹/₄ cup lowfat milk, plus more if needed
1¹/₂ teaspoons vanilla extract

Combine the sugar and cocoa in a small bowl. In another small bowl, beat the margarine. Add the sugar mixture alternately with the milk, and beat to a spreading consistency, adding additional milk if needed. Beat in the vanilla.
MAKES ABOUT 2 CUPS

Nutritional Analysis per Serving (cake with frosting):
Calories, 380; Fiber, 3 gm; Cholesterol, 19.5 mg.; Sodium, 560 mg.
% Calories from: Protein, 5%; Carbohydrate, 78%; Fat, 17% (7.5 gm)

NOTE: Original recipe contains 464 calories, 55 milligrams cholesterol, and 18 grams of fat per serving. ·

Three-Step Cheesecake

I like my cheesecake at least an inch and a half high, so I use one and a half times the ingedients in the original recipe. You could also do the math to get a cheesecake around two inches high. The original recipe uses Kraft's Philadelphia brand cream cheese, and I still think it's the best. I added a little lemon zest for more flavor.

GRAHAM CRACKER CRUST

2 tablespoons butter or margarine, melted

2 tablespoons low-fat sweetened condensed milk

1 tablespoon Kahlúa, light Bailey's Irish cream or other liqueur, or 1 tablespoon milk

2 tablespoons sugar

1¼ cups finely crushed graham crackers (about 18 crackers)

FILLING

2 8-ounce packages Philadelphia brand light cream cheese, softened

1 8-ounce package Philadelphia brand fat-free cream cheese, softened

¾ cup sugar

1½ teaspoons vanilla extract

1 large egg

⅓ cup fat-free egg substitute

Finely chopped zest of 1 lemon

To make the crust, coat a 9-inch pie plate or springform pan with nonstick cooking spray. In a medium bowl, stir together the butter, condensed milk, Kahlúa, and sugar. Add the graham crackers and toss to mix well. Press the mixture evenly into the bottom of the prepared pan. Chill for about 1 hour, or until firm. (Or bake in a preheated 375-degree oven for 4 minutes. Cool on a wire rack before filling.)

Preheat the oven to 350 degrees. In a large bowl, mix the cream cheeses, sugar, and vanilla with an electric mixer on medium speed until well blended. Add the egg and egg substitute; mix until well blended. Stir in the lemon zest. Pour into the crust.

Bake for 40 minutes, or until the center is almost set. Cool. Refrigerate for at least 3 hours, or overnight.

Makes 12 servings

Nutritional Analysis per Serving:
Calories, 244; Fiber 0.3 gm; Cholesterol, 41 mg; Sodium, 396 mg % Calories from: Protein, 16%; Carbohydrate, 49%; Fat, 35% (9 gm)

NOTE: Original recipe contains 373 calories, 117 milligrams cholesterol, and 23 grams of fat per serving.

Red Velvet Cake (also known as Waldorf Astoria Cake or $1000 Cake)

The leavening in this cake comes from the air you beat into it, as well as from the reaction between the baking soda and the buttermilk, so be sure your batter is nice and fluffy.

¼ cup butter flavor shortening
¼ cup fat-free cream cheese
1½ cups sugar
1 large egg plus ¼ cup fat-free egg substitute (or use 2 large eggs)
2 1-ounce bottles red food coloring
¼ cup unsweetened cocoa
2 teaspoons vanilla extract
1 teaspoon baking soda
1 teaspoon salt
1 teaspoon vinegar
1 cup low-fat buttermilk
2¼ cups all-purpose flour

BUTTER FROSTING
2 tablespoons butter, softened
2 tablespoons fat-free cream cheese, softened
3 cups confectioners' sugar
2 tablespoons milk, plus more if necessary
1 teaspoon vanilla extract

Preheat the oven to 350 degrees. Coat two 8-inch round cake pans with nonstick cooking spray. In a large bowl, cream the shortening and cream cheese together until fluffy. Add the sugar, egg, and egg substitute and beat until light and fluffy. Beat in the food coloring, cocoa, and vanilla extract.

Add the soda, salt, and vinegar to the buttermilk and mix thoroughly. Add this mixture, in thirds, alternately with the flour, to the shortening mixture, beating thoroughly after each addition. Split the batter between the prepared pans. Bake for 30 minutes or until a toothpick inserted in the center comes out clean. Let the cake layers cool slightly in the pans, then remove them from the pans and let them cool completely on wire racks.

To make the frosting, in a medium bowl, beat the butter and cream cheese until soft and fluffy. Gradually add 1½ cups of the powdered sugar, beating well. Slowly beat in the milk and vanilla. Slowly beat in the remaining sugar. Beat in additional milk if needed to make the frosting spreadable. Cover and refrigerate until needed.

MAKES 12 SERVINGS

Nutritional Analysis per Serving:
Calories, 360; Cholesterol, 33 mg; Sodium 400 mg
% Calories from: Protein, 4%; Carbohydrate, 76%; Fat, 20% (8 gm)

NOTE: Original recipe contains 567 calories, 64 milligrams cholesterol, and 35 grams of fat per serving.

Chocolate Coffee Cheesecake

This luscious but lower-fat version of the Kahlúa company's recipe for Chocolate Kahlúa Cheesecake is decadently rich in chocolate flavor, accented by the coffee liqueur, but has only a third of the fat grams of the original.

CHOCOLATE COOKIE CRUST

1½ cups SnackWell's reduced-fat chocolate sandwich cookie
    crumbs (about 14 cookies) or reduced-fat Oreos
    (ground with food processor)
3 tablespoons chocolate syrup
1 tablespoon Kahlúa
1 tablespoon all-purpose flour

¾ cup (4½ ounces) semisweet chocolate chips
¼ cup evaporated skim milk
¼ cup Kahlúa
12 ounces Philadelphia light cream cheese
12 ounces Philadelphia free (fat-free) cream cheese
1 cup sugar
⅓ cup unsweetened cocoa
1 large egg
⅓ cup fat-free egg substitute
1 teaspoon vanilla extract

TOPPING
⅔ cup (4 ounces) semisweet chocolate chips
2 tablespoons chocolate syrup
2 tablespoons Kahlúa

Light Cool Whip for garnish (optional)
12 chocolate candy kisses for garnish (optional)

Preheat the oven to 350 degrees. Spray a 9-inch springform pan with nonstick cooking spray. To make the crust, combine the chocolate cookie crumbs, chocolate syrup, and Kahlúa in a food processor and process to blend (or combine in a bowl and stir together with a fork). Pour the cookie mixture into the prepared pan and spread evenly. Sprinkle the top with the flour. Press cookie mixture over the bottom and one-third of the way up the sides of the pan to form a crust. Freeze for 5 minutes.

Bake the crust for 10 minutes. Let cool. Increase the oven temperature to 400 degrees.

Place the chocolate chips in a microwave-safe bowl or glass measuring cup. Microwave on High for 1 minute, or until melted. Stir until smooth. Add the evaporated milk and the Kahlúa and stir until blended.

In a large bowl, beat both cream cheeses and the sugar until fluffy. Add the cocoa; beat until blended. Add the egg and egg substitute, beating well after each addition. Stir in the vanilla and the reserved chocolate mixture. Pour into the prepared crust.

Bake for 10 minutes, then reduce the oven temperature to 275 degrees and bake for 45 minutes. Let cool. Loosen the cake from the edges of the pan with a dinner knife and remove the springform ring.

To make the topping, place the chocolate chips in a micro-wave-safe bowl. Microwave on High for 1 minute, or until melted. Stir until smooth. Stir in the chocolate syrup and Kahlúa; blend well. Spread the topping over the top of the cake with a spoon. Refrigerate for at least 6 hours.

At serving time, garnish each slice with a dollop of Cool Whip and a chocolate kiss if desired.

MAKES 12 SERVINGS

Nutritional Analysis per Serving:
Calories 385; Fiber, 2 gm; Cholesterol, 30 mg; Sodium, 443 mg
% Calories from: Protein, 11%; Carbohydrate, 57%; Fat, 32% (14 gm)

NOTE: Original recipe contains 609 calories, 157 milligrams cholesterol, and 44 grams of fat per serving.

Chapter 8

Pies and Other Desserts

Rice Cereal Treats

The original recipe for Rice Krispies Treats is actually pretty low in fat, but my version manages to trim off another couple of grams!

2 tablespoons butter or margarine
1 10-ounce package regular marshmallows (about 40) or
4 cups miniature marshmallows
6 cups Kellogg's Rice Krispies

Coat a 9-inch square baking pan with nonstick cooking spray. Melt the butter or margarine in a large nonstick saucepan over low heat. Spray the sides of the pan with nonstick cooking spray. Add the marshmallows and stir until completely melted. Remove from the heat. Add the Rice Krispies and stir until well coated.

Using a spatula (or a square of waxed paper) that has been coated with nonstick cooking spray, press the mixture evenly into the prepared pan. Let cool, then cut into squares. For crunchy treats, keep in the refrigerator.

MAKES 12 TREATS

MICROWAVE DIRECTIONS:

In a microwave-safe glass mixing bowl that has been coated with nonstick cooking spray, microwave the butter and marshmallows at High for 2 minutes. Stir to blend. Microwave at High for 1 minute longer. Stir until smooth. Add the cereal. Stir until well coated. Press into the pan as directed above and let cool.

Nutritional Analysis per Treat:
Calories, 149; Fiber, 0.2 gm; Cholesterol, 5 mg; Sodium, 203 mg
% Calories from: Protein, 4%; Carbohydrate, 84%; Fat, 12% (2 gm)

NOTE: Original recipe contains 166 calories and 4 grams of fat per treat.

Pumpkin Pie

The classic pumpkin pie on the label of Libby's canned pumpkin puree has probably appeared on millions of Thanksgiving tables over the years. By using egg substitute and evaporated skimmed milk, and a light piecrust, I've eliminated half the fat grams but saved the rich, spicy taste.

½ cup fat-free egg substitute
1 16-ounce can Libby's solid-pack pumpkin
¾ cup sugar
1 teaspoon ground cinnamon
½ teaspoon ground ginger
¼ teaspoon ground cloves
½ teaspoon salt
1 12-ounce can undiluted Carnation evaporated skimmed
*   milk (see first Note)*
1½ teaspoons grated orange zest (optional)
1 unbaked 9-inch Light and Flaky Piecrust (page 223)

Preheat the oven to 425 degrees. In a large bowl, combine the egg substitute, pumpkin, sugar, cinnamon, ginger, cloves, salt, and evaporated milk and beat just until smooth. Stir in the orange zest if desired. Pour into the prepared piecrust.

Bake for 15 minutes (if using a metal or foil pan, bake on a preheated heavy-duty baking sheet). Reduce the oven temperature to 350 degrees; bake for 40 minutes longer, or until a knife inserted near the center comes out clean. Cool on a wire rack.

MAKES 10 SERVINGS

NOTE: If you like, substitute 2 tablespoons dark rum for 2 tablespoons of the evaporated milk.

Nutritional Analysis per Serving:
Calories, 171; Fiber, 1.3 gm; Cholesterol, 7.5 mg; Sodium, 180 mg
% Calories from: Protein, 15%; Carbohydrate, 49%; Fat, 36% (7 gm)

NOTE: Original recipe contains 232 calories, 53 milligrams cholesterol, and 14.5 grams of fat per serving.

Coffee Pecan Pie

The original recipe for this pecan pie appears in a booklet of recipes put out by Kahlúa. I've kept the crisp chocolate crust and gooey, nut-studded filling while eliminating more than half the fat and a third of the cholesterol.

1 tablespoon butter, softened
¼ cup fat-free cream cheese, softened
¾ cup sugar
2 teaspoons vanilla extract
2 tablespoons all-purpose flour
1 large egg
½ cup fat-free egg substitute
½ cup Kahlúa
½ cup dark corn syrup
¾ cup evaporated skim milk
¾ cup whole or chopped pecans
Chocolate Cookie Crust (page 196), prepared in a 9-inch pie
*   plate*
Light Cool Whip or light whipped cream and pecan halves
*   for garnish (optional)*

Preheat the oven to 325 degrees. In a large bowl, beat together the butter, cream cheese, sugar, vanilla, and flour. Beat in the egg, then beat in the egg substitute ¼ cup at a time. Stir in the Kahlúa, corn syrup, evaporated milk, and pecans. Mix well. Pour into the prepared pie crust.

Bake for about 40 minutes, or until set. Let cool, then chill. Garnish, if desired, with Cool Whip and pecan halves.
Makes 10 servings

Nutritional Analysis per Serving:
Calories, 335; Fiber, 1.2 gm; Cholesterol, 25 mg; Sodium, 168 mg
% Calories from: Protein, 8%; Carbohydrate, 68%; Fat, 24%
(9 gm)

NOTE: Original recipe contains 410 calories, 82 milligrams cholesterol, and 22 grams of fat per serving.

Chocolate–Peanut Butter Cereal Snack Mix

Chex Muddy Buddies are a hit with every kid (and many of the grown-ups) that I know. I've lightened up the fat and calorie counts in this version so you don't have to feel quite as guilty when you indulge.

> 9 cups of your favorite Chex brand cereals (corn, rice, and/
>   or wheat)
> ⅔ cup Hershey's semisweet chocolate chips
> ½ cup reduced-fat creamy peanut butter, such as Jif
> 1 tablespoon butter or margarine
> ¼ cup chocolate syrup
> 1½ teaspoons vanilla extract
> 1½ cups C&H confectioners' Sugar

Pour the cereals into a large bowl; set aside. In a 1-quart microwave-safe bowl, combine the chocolate chips, peanut butter, butter, and chocolate syrup. Microwave on High for 1 to 1½ minutes, or until smooth, stirring after 1 minute. Stir in the vanilla. Let cool for 1 minute.

Pour the chocolate mixture over the cereals, stirring until evenly coated. Pour the cereal mixture into a large resealable plastic bag, add the confectioners' sugar, and seal securely. Shake until all the pieces are well coated. Spread on waxed paper to cool.
Makes 9 cups

Nutritional Analysis per ½ Cup:
Calories, 166; Fiber, 1 gm; Cholesterol, 2 mg; Sodium, 172 mg
% Calories from: Protein, 6%; Carbohydrate, 64%; Fat, 29%
(5.7 gm)

NOTE: Original recipe contains 200 calories, 7 milligrams cholesterol, and 10 grams of fat per ½-cup serving.

STOVETOP METHOD: Heat the chocolate chips, peanut butter, butter, and chocolate syrup in a small saucepan over low heat, stirring often, until smooth. Remove from the heat; stir in the vanilla. Proceed as directed above.

Easy Eggless Key Lime Pie

I kept hearing about the wonderful Key lime pies they have in Florida from my best friend, who now lives there. Even though today you are more likely to see Key lime pie made with a graham cracker crust and a whipped cream topping, the original version was apparently made with a pastry crust and a meringue top. I like to take the best of both versions and prepare it with a low-fat cookie crust and a fat-free meringue topping. Just in case you like it the other ways, there are directions below for using the Light and Flaky Piecrust and lower-fat whipped cream or light Cool Whip instead of the meringue. But you know what? Whichever way you make it, limes never tasted so good.

2 envelopes (scant 2 tablespoons) unflavored gelatin
1/2 cup water
2 14-ounce cans Eagle low-fat sweetened condensed milk
1 cup bottled Key lime juice or other bottled lime juice
Grated zest of 1 to 2 limes (optional)
1 Caramel-Pecan Cookie Crust (recipe follows) or 1 baked
*   9-inch Light and Flaky Piecrust (page 223)*
Whipped Cream Topping (see below), light Cool Whip, or
*   Meringue Topping (see below)*

Blend the gelatin with the water in a small nonstick saucepan and let sit for 1 minute. Then cook over medium-low heat, stirring constantly, until the gelatin dissolves and the mixture is clear. Set aside to cool.

Pour the condensed milk into a large bowl. Slowly stir in the lime juice and continue to stir mixture gently until it thickens, a few minutes. Fold in the gelatin mixture and the lime zest and stir to blend well. Spread in the prepared pie shell. Refrigerate for at least 3 hours.

Top the pie with whipped cream, Cool Whip, or meringue. If topping with meringue, spread it on top of the chilled pie and place the pie briefly under the broiler to lightly brown the meringue. Chill until ready to serve.

MAKES 12 SERVINGS

Nutritional Analysis per Serving (with Caramel-Pecan Cookie Crust and no topping):
Calories, 295; Fiber, 0.3 gm; Cholesterol, 10.5 mg; Sodium, 122 mg
% Calories from: Protein, 10%; Carbohydrate, 72%; Fat, 18% (6 gm)

NOTE: Original recipe calls for half as much filling but serves 8 instead of 12; it contains 310 calories, 120 milligrams cholesterol, and 17 grams of fat per serving.

Caramel-Pecan Cookie Crust

1 tablespoon butter
1 tablespoon milk
2 tablespoons Kahlúa
3 tablespoons sugar
28 reduced-fat vanilla wafers
¼ cup pecan pieces

Spray a 9-inch deep-dish pie plate with nonstick cooking spray. In a small nonstick saucepan, blend the butter, milk, Kahlúa, and sugar. Cook over low heat, stirring continuously, for 2 minutes. Remove from the heat.

In a food processor, combine the vanilla wafers and pecan pieces and process to crumbs. Pour in the butter mixture and pulse briefly to blend. While the mixture is still warm, press over the bottom and 1½ inches up the sides of the prepared pie pan. It is easiest to press the crumb mixture into the pan using the back of a large spoon that has been sprayed with nonstick cooking spray; spray the spoon several times during the process.

Meringue Topping

4 egg whites
¼ teaspoon cream of tartar
6 tablespoons sugar

In a large bowl, beat the egg whites until soft peaks form. Add the cream of tartar and then the sugar, a tablespoon at a time, and beat until fairly stiff. (This will add 29 calories per serving.)

Whipped Cream Topping

¾ cup heavy cream
Confectioners' sugar to taste (optional)

Beat the cream until stiff. Add confectioners' sugar to taste, if desired. Top each serving with 2 tablespoons whipped cream. (This will add 19 calories and 1.6 grams of fat per serving.)

Baked Key Lime Pie

This Key lime pie recipe is for the cooks who prefer to make dishes the old-fashioned way.

4 large egg yolks
¼ cup fat-free egg substitute
2 14-ounce cans Eagle low-fat sweetened condensed milk
1 cup bottled Key lime juice or other bottled real lime juice
Green food coloring (optional)
1 baked 9- or 10-inch Light and Flaky Piecrust (page 223)
    or 1 deep-dish 9-inch Caramel-Pecan Cookie Crust
    (page 209)
Meringue Topping (page 210) or Whipped Cream Topping
    (page 210)

Preheat the oven to 350 degrees. In a large bowl, beat the egg yolks, egg substitute, and condensed milk until creamy. Slowly fold in the lime juice and continue to fold until the mixture thickens, a few minutes. Fold in about 8 drops of green food coloring if desired. Pour into the prepared pie shell.

Bake for about 12 minutes. If using meringue, spread it over the hot pie filling, spreading it to the edges of the pie plate. Bake until golden brown, about 15 minutes. Let cool, then refrigerate. If using whipped cream, let the pie cool, chill, and then top with the cream. Refrigerate leftovers.
MAKES 12 SERVINGS

Nutritional Analysis per Serving (made with Light and Flaky Piecrust and not including topping):
Calories, 326; Fiber, 0.5 gm; Cholesterol, 79 mg; Sodium, 176 mg
% Calories from: Protein, 10%; Carbohydrate, 63%; Fat, 27% (9.8 gm)

NOTE: Original recipe contains 382 calories, 128 milligrams cholesterol, and 16 grams of fat per serving.

Flan

This is my best friend's favorite dessert. And flan is quite popular in many areas around the world—including California, where I live.

¾ cup sugar
4 large eggs
1 large egg white or 2 tablespoons fat-free egg substitute
1 tablespoon vanilla extract
1 14-ounce can low-fat sweetened condensed milk
1¾ cups 1% milk
¼ cup fat-free cream cheese, softened

Preheat the oven to 350 degrees. Place the sugar in the top of a double boiler and set over boiling water. Cook until the sugar liquefies and turns a walnut-brown color, stirring frequently with a wooden spoon. Watch carefully so that the sugar doesn't burn. Pour the caramel (melted sugar) into a 9-inch flan pan or soufflé dish and quickly tilt the pan to coat the bottom.

Place the eggs, egg white, vanilla, both milks, and the cream cheese in a blender or food processor and process for about 5 minutes, or until smooth. Pour the mixture into the prepared pan and place in a larger baking pan. Pour in enough boiling water to come halfway up the sides of the flan pan. Cover the top of the flan pan with foil if you want to prevent the top of the flan from turning dark brown.

Bake for 1 hour to 1 hour and 10 minutes, or until a knife inserted in the center comes out clean. Remove from the water bath and let cool to room temperature.

To serve, run a knife around the edge of the flan and invert the custard onto a deep serving plate. Serve each piece with some of the caramel syrup.

MAKES 6 TO 8 SERVINGS

Nutritional Analysis per Serving (8 servings per recipe):
Calories, 290; Cholesterol, 114 mg; Sodium, 156 mg
% Calories from: Protein, 15%; Carbohydrate, 70%; Fat, 15%
(4.8 gm)

NOTE: Original recipe contains 340 calories, 191 milligrams cholesterol, and 13 grams of fat per serving.

Crème Brûlée

Crème brûlée usually uses heavy whipping cream to make the custard. And, even then, the directions warn, "do not boil" the egg-cream mixture. If you *do* boil it, the mixture curdles and the water separates out (not very appetizing). Well, lower-fat creams and milks aren't as forgiving as heavy cream—so it becomes even more important to avoid boiling. I found that using a double boiler works best, keeping the heat at a medium simmer. The custard will start to coat the spoon right around the fifteen-minute mark. To guarantee a firmer texture, I also added a package of gelatin into the equation.

1½ cups half-and-half
1½ cups evaporated skim milk
1 egg
4 egg yolks
⅓ cup granulated sugar
1 package (scant 1 tablespoon) unflavored gelatin blended
*   with 2 tablespoons cold water*
2 teaspoons vanilla extract

FOR RASPBERRY CRÈME BRÛLÉE (OPTIONAL)
¼ cup Grand Marnier or other liqueur of choice
¼ cup granulated sugar
½ cup frozen raspberries

⅓ cup packed brown sugar

In a 1-quart saucepan, heat the half-and-half and milk over medium heat until tiny bubbles form around the edge of the pan.

Meanwhile, start heating water in the bottom of a double boiler. In the top of the pan, blend the egg, yolks, and sugar with a wire whisk.

Slowly stir the hot milk mixture into the eggs. Keeping the water in the bottom of the double boiler at a medium simmer, cook the custard mixture, stirring constantly, for 10 minutes. Stir in the gelatin mixture and continue to cook and stir until the mixture just coats the back of a metal spoon, about 5 minutes more—DO NOT BOIL. Stir in the vanilla. Set aside.

If using the raspberries, place the Grand Marnier in a small bowl and the sugar in another small bowl. Dunk about 1 tablespoon of the still-frozen raspberries at a time in the Grand Marnier, then set them in the sugar to coat. Place the raspberries in the bottom of 8 custard cups or in the bottom of a 1½-quart broiler-safe casserole.

Pour the custard mixture carefully into the custard cups or casserole and refrigerate until well chilled, about 6 hours.

Sift the brown sugar over the chilled custard. Place under the broiler for 3 to 4 minutes, until the sugar melts. Refrigerate until ready to serve.

MAKES 8 SERVINGS

Nutritional Analysis per Serving:
Calories, 204; Cholesterol, 151 mg; Sodium, 88 mg
% Calories from: Protein, 15%; Carbohydrate, 48%; Fat, 37% (8.5 gm)

NOTE: Original recipe contains 412 calories, 255 milligrams cholesterol, and 36 grams of fat per serving.

Lemon Meringue Pie

Light and luscious lemon meringue pie gets even lighter but stays just as luscious in my version of the classic recipe.

> 1 cup sugar
> 5 tablespoons Argo or Kingsford's cornstarch
> 1½ cups cold water
> 2 large egg yolks, slightly beaten
> 2 tablespoons fat-free egg substitute
> Grated zest of 1 lemon
> 5 tablespoons lemon juice
> 1½ teaspoons Mazola margarine
> 2 drops yellow food coloring (optional)
> 1 baked 9-inch Light and Flaky Piecrust (page 223)

> MERINGUE TOPPING
> 3 large egg whites
> ⅓ cup sugar

Preheat the oven to 350 degrees. In a medium nonstick saucepan, combine the sugar and cornstarch. Gradually stir in the water until smooth. Stir in the egg yolks and egg substitute. Stirring constantly, bring to a boil over medium heat and boil for 1 minute. Remove from the heat and stir in the lemon zest, lemon juice, margarine, and the food coloring, if desired. Spoon the hot filling into the prepared piecrust.

In a small bowl, with an electric mixer on high speed, beat the egg whites until foamy. Gradually beat in the sugar; continue beating until stiff peaks form. Spread the meringue evenly over hot filling, sealing the edge of the crust.

Bake for 15 to 20 minutes, or until the meringue is golden. Cool on a wire rack; refrigerate.

MAKES 8 SERVINGS

MICROWAVE DIRECTIONS: In a large microwave-safe bowl, combine the sugar and cornstarch. Gradually stir in the water until smooth. Stir in the egg yolks and egg substitute. Microwave on High, stirring twice with a wire whisk, for 6 to 8 minutes, or until the mixture boils; boil for 1 minute. Stir in the lemon zest, lemon juice, margarine, and food coloring if desired. Spoon the hot filling into the piecrust and continue as directed above.

Nutritional Analysis per Serving:
Calories, 327; Fiber, 0.6 gm; Cholesterol, 55 mg; Sodium, 177 mg % Calories from: Protein, 6%; Carbohydrate, 66%; Fat, 28% (10 gm)

NOTE: Original recipe contains 375 calories, 83 milligrams cholesterol, and 17 grams of fat per serving

Tiramisù

This is one of those recipes that ends up turning your kitchen upside down—you know the type. You go about your business, following the recipe step by step. After you finish it and place your masterpiece in the refrigerator, you turn around only to find you've used every pot and pan and appliance in your kitchen. Your reward? About twenty minutes of dishwashing duty. But you know what? It's worth it. I have yet to meet a person who doesn't love this tiramisù.

CUSTARD FILLING
2 large egg yolks
2 tablespoons fat-free egg substitute
¼ cup sugar
⅓ cup sauterne wine or sherry
2 cups light Cool Whip or ½ cup heavy cream, whipped

1 cup brewed espresso or other strong coffee (instant is okay)

MASCARPONE FILLING
½ cup light or fat-free cream cheese
⅓ cup low-fat ricotta cheese
2 tablespoons light corn syrup
2 tablespoons confectioners' sugar
2 tablespoons all-purpose flour
¼ teaspoon vanilla extract
1 cup light Cool Whip
3 tablespoons reserved espresso (see above)

ORANGE SAUCE
Finely chopped zest of 2 oranges
6 tablespoons orange juice
5 tablespoons sugar
¼ cup Grand Marnier

Cocoa or grated sweet chocolate for garnish

First, make the custard filling: Place the egg yolks and fat-free egg substitute in the top of a double boiler. Whisk in the sugar, then whisk in the wine. Whisk for about 30 seconds, then set over gently boiling water (make sure the water does not touch the bottom of the top pan). Whisk until the mixture expands to about 1½ times its volume, about 3 to 5 minutes, then cook for several minutes longer, still whisking, until the mixture thickens. (If it sticks to the whisk when the whisk is lifted from the pan, it is done.) Do not overwhisk or the custard will lose lightness. Refrigerate until completely cool. Then fold in the Cool Whip. Keep in the refrigerator until needed.

To make the mascarpone filling: In a mini-processor, blend the cream cheese, ricotta, corn syrup, confectioners' sugar, flour, and vanilla until smooth. Spoon into a medium bowl and fold in the Cool Whip and 3 tablespoons espresso. Keep in the refrigerator until needed.

To make the orange sauce: Place the orange zest, orange juice, and sugar in a small saucepan and cook over low heat for 10 minutes. Set aside to cool, then stir in the Grand Marnier. Set aside.

To assemble: Dip each slice of cake or each slab of ladyfingers ever so lightly in the espresso, then place in the bottom of a 9-inch square baking dish. Once the bottom of the pan is completely covered, drizzle about a third of the orange sauce, teaspoon by teaspoon, evenly over the cake. Spread about two-thirds of the mascarpone filling over the cake. Top with another cake or ladyfinger layer (remember to dip lightly in the espresso) and drizzle with orange sauce. Top with two-thirds of the custard filling. Repeat with the remaining cake and espresso, orange sauce, and mascarpone. Top with the remaining custard sauce. Sift cocoa or sprinkle chocolate over the top. Refrigerate and let set for at least 4 hours or up to a day.

MAKES 9 LARGE OR 12 SMALL SERVINGS

Nutritional Analysis per Large Serving (based on 2¹/₂ packages ladyfingers):

Calories, 333; Cholesterol, 56 mg; Sodium, 230 mg

% Calories from: Protein, 9%; Carbohydrate, 74%; Fat, 17% (6.4 gm)

NOTE: Original recipe contains approximately 575 calories, 290 milligrams cholesterol, and 36 grams of fat per large serving.

Black-Bottom Cupcakes

I tested these cupcakes out on my Jazzercise class and the teacher told me that everybody loved them so much I should patent the recipe. Several of the people also told me these tasted better than the higher-fat versions they had had—imagine that!

CREAM CHEESE FILLING
3/4 cup fat-free cream cheese, softened
1 teaspoon vanilla extract
1/3 cup plus 1 tablespoon sugar
1 large egg
1/3 cup (2 ounces) semisweet chocolate chips
1/3 cup (2 ounces) milk chocolate chips

1 1/2 cups all-purpose or unbleached all-purpose flour
1 cup sugar
1/4 cup unsweetened cocoa
1 teaspoon baking soda
1/2 teaspoon salt
1 cup water
2 tablespoons canola oil
3 tablespoons light sour cream
1 tablespoon vinegar
1 1/2 teaspoons vanilla extract
1/3 cup chopped almonds (optional)
2 tablespoons sugar (optional)

Preheat the oven to 350 degrees. Line 18 muffin cups with foil or paper baking cups. To make the cream cheese filling, in a small bowl, beat the cream cheese, vanilla, sugar, and egg until smooth. Stir in the chocolate chips; set aside.

In a large bowl, combine the flour, sugar, cocoa, baking soda, and salt; mix well. Add the water, oil, sour cream, vinegar, and vanilla; using an electric mixer, beat for 2 minutes on medium speed.

Fill the muffin cups half-full with the batter. Top each with a tablespoonful of the cream cheese mixture. Sprinkle chopped almonds and sugar over the top if desired.

Bake for 20 minutes, or until the cream cheese mixture is light golden brown. Cool for 15 mintues; remove from the pans. Cool completely. Store in the refrigerator.

MAKES 18 CUPCAKES

Nutritional Analysis per Cupcake:
Calories, 161; Fiber, 1 gm; Cholesterol, 12 mg; Sodium, 172 mg
% Calories from: Protein, 9%; Carbohydrate, 70%; Fat, 21% (4.4 gm)

NOTE: Original recipe contains 250 calories, 25 milligrams cholesterol, and 13 grams of fat per serving.

Light and Flaky Piecrust

The piecrust recipe on packages of Crisco is still one of the best around. By replacing some of the shortening with fat-free cream cheese and low-fat buttermilk, I've cut down on the calories and fat without sacrificing taste or texture.

1⅓ cups sifted all-purpose flour
½ teaspoon salt
5 tablespoons butter-flavor Crisco
3 tablespoons fat-free cream cheese
3 to 4 tablespoons low-fat buttermilk

Combine the flour and salt in a medium bowl. With a pastry blender or two knives, cut in the Crisco and cream cheese until uniform; the mixture should resemble coarse meal. Sprinkle with the buttermilk, a tablespoon at a time, and toss with a fork just until the dough comes together. Knead in any dry crumbs.

On a lightly floured surface, roll the dough into a circle to fit a 9-inch pie plate. Gently ease the dough into the plate (you may have to use a spatula to lift up the dough). Trim the dough to ½ inch beyond the edge of the plate; fold under to make a double thickness of dough around rim and flute with your fingers or crimp with a fork.

For a prebaked crust, prick the bottom and sides thoroughly with a fork. Bake at 425 degrees for 10 to 15 minutes, or until golden.

Nutritional Analysis per Serving (12 servings per recipe):
Calories, 100; Fiber, 0.4 gm; Cholesterol, 0 mg; Sodium, 95 mg
% Calories from: Protein, 6%; Carbohydrate, 44%; Fat, 50% (5.5 gm)

NOTE: Original recipe contains 126 calories and 8.8 grams of fat per serving.

Index

Hershey's kiss, fat and calorie cost of, 33
Hollandaise Sauce, 106
Honey-Roasted Party Mix, 74

I Can't Believe It's Not Butter, 41
Icing, 99
ingredients, best-tasting and freshest, 13
Italian:
  Focaccia, Quick, 91
  Focaccia, Yeast, with Tomato and Cheese, 93
  herb and spice blend, 40
  Hero Sandwiches, 109
  Tiramisù, 218

jam, fat and calorie cost of, 33
Japanese herb and spice blend, 41
jelly-roll pans, 24

Kahlúa, 8
  Chocolate Kahlúa Cheesecake, lighter version of, 196
  Pecan Pie, lighter version of, 204
Kellogg's, 8
Kentucky Fried Chicken (KFC):
  chicken, lighter version of, 113
  coleslaw, lighter version of, 53
Kessler, John, 5
Key lime pies:
  Baked, 211
  Easy Eggless, 208
Kraft, 8

lemon:
  Butter Frosting, 183
  Chiffon Cake, 182
  juice, 27
  Meringue Pie, 216
  Squares, Low-Fat, 165
Libby:
  Pumpkin Pecan Bread, lighter version of, 83
  Pumpkin Pie, lighter version of, 202
lime pies, see Key lime pies
Lipton, 8

Lord, Jane, 5
low-fat cooking, 13–50
  "baking extras" and, 29–31
  cheesecake makeover, 3, 43–48
  Chicago-Style Pizza makeover, 3, 43–48
  Chocolate Mocha Mousse makeover, 48–50
  cocoa-chocolate swap and, 31–34
  cooking methods in, 18–20
  egg substitutes in, 36–37
  egg whites in, 34–36
  filo in, 37–39
  food tools in, 26–29
  herbs and spices in, 39–41
  ideal fat threshold in, 13, 20–22
  keys to success in, 16–17
  kitchen tools in, 23–25
  table tips and tricks in, 41–42
  tips and tricks in, 29–42
  see also fat replacements

macaroni:
  and Cheese, 116
  Salad, Creamy, 71
Magic Cookie Bars, 163
main dishes, see entrées
M&M's, fat and calorie cost of, 32
maple syrup, 27
margarine, 41
marinades, 15
  ideal fat thresholds and fat replacements for, 22
Marinara Sauce, 124
marshmallows:
  as "baking extra," 31
  fat and calorie cost of, 33
  Magic Cookie Bars, 163
  Rice Cereal Treats, 201
mascarpone cheese:
  Filling, 218
  replacement for, 16–17
mayonnaise, 18, 42
  fat-free, reduced-fat, or light, 27
  lower-fat replacement for, 29
measuring spoons, 24–25
Meatballs, Sweet 'n' Sour, 76